REFLECTIONS ON A

LESSONS

CAREER SPENT IN IRELAND'S

FROM THE

CRIMINAL COURTS

BENCH

Judge Gillian Hussey

GILL BOOKS

Gill Books
Hume Avenue
Park West
Dublin 12
www.gillbooks.ie

Gill Books is an imprint of M.H. Gill and Co.

978 07171 9268 7

Designed by Typo•glyphix, Burton-on-Trent, DE14 3HE
Edited by Rachel Pierce
Copyedited by Sands Publishing Solutions
Proofread by Ciara McNee

Printed by Clays Ltd, Suffolk
This book is typeset in 12 on 20pt, Sabon.

*The paper used in this book comes from the wood pulp
of sustainably managed forests.*

5 4 3 2 1

To my children,
Ronan, Caitriona and Duncan;
and also my grandchildren,
Karl, Emma, Leah, Zoë and Jack

ACKNOWLEDGEMENTS

I think as you hit old age, there is a fork in the path: one way leads to gratitude, the other to regrets. Hopefully the road more travelled is that towards gratitude. It's certainly my preferred path. As I survey my life to date – my career, my personal choices – I'm struck by the debt of gratitude I owe to so many people.

I've been extremely lucky throughout my life, starting with my uncle's stewardship of my career. My uncle, Anthony Hussey, prepared me for a life in the law and it was thanks to him that I was able to take the opportunities granted to me and make the most of them. I owe him so much.

In the traditional Acknowledgements section, you find a long list of names of all those who have helped the author in some way. I have wrestled with this throughout the long process of writing this book. The problem is, my wonderful memory is now not what it used to be, and names can elude me – especially as I met so many, many people over the course of 18 years on the bench. I became extremely worried about listing out names and, inevitably, forgetting some in the process – a thought that unnerves me. So I will ask everyone to whom I owe thanks to forgive me for not listing out the names here. I would hate to cause offence, so I think my best approach is not to start a list that I can't properly finish.

That said, I would like to acknowledge that it takes teamwork to run a court well – and a very big team at that. I am immensely grateful to every single person who helped me to run my court and conduct my cases and judgments. In my work, I relied heavily on the registrars, the probation officers and the gardaí to do their jobs well and to help me to do mine well. They were honourable, hardworking, humorous people, and I relished their company as much as their professionalism. When I look back now, we were working in such difficult circumstances: never enough resources, never enough time, hearing stories of such sadness and tragedy, but the whole court pulled together as a team to keep the show on the road day in, day out. It was no mean feat.

Every registrar I worked with was superb, I have to say, and I couldn't have done my day's work without them. The probation officers so impressed me with their devotion to their work and their quiet fortitude in the face of mammoth caseloads and often minimal resources. The victims of crime who braved the courtroom always had my sympathy and I hope they felt well treated in my court. Those who had committed crimes were a very mixed bunch, but they were all people who had made mistakes and bad choices, and many of them were courageous enough to face up to that and to try to make changes. Those who engaged with the available services and turned their lives around have my undying admiration. Nothing has ever given me greater satisfaction than attending graduations at treatment centres and observing these rehabilitated citizens finally taking their place in society. It is a delight on a personal and on a societal level. That is why I'm so heartily glad that I met Aubrey McCarthy and became involved with Tiglin, as a patron, and with Fr Denis Laverty at St James's Camino Network. As is so often the case in these centres, Fr Denis is surrounded by likeminded people, many of whom have come through his addiction programme and are now devoted to helping others. I'm in awe of the work done by all these essential organisations that extend a helping hand. Their work is the backbone of good society.

I must also acknowledge the wonderful work and perseverance of Crime Victims Helpline, of which I remain a patron. These services are staffed by absolutely brilliant people, and our world would be much poorer without them. The only problem is that there are never enough of them – but those who are there deserve our gratitude.

As I have said so often before, the gardaí I worked with were and remain great friends. I was indebted to them for their professionalism, their insights and their great sense of humour. I could never thank them individually, so a broad and heartfelt thank you will have to suffice. I know they know that I admire them hugely for working so hard for the safety and security of us all. They were essential to my work, and I am so grateful to one and all for that. I must just mention two retired members because they helped with details for this book – Tony Hickey and Feargal Foley, thank you.

My many wonderful friendships have sustained me throughout my life, and I thank all of my friends for that. They might never know just how valuable their contribution to my life has been.

I would also like to acknowledge the love and support of my family, to whom this book is dedicated. And I would like to thank those not included in the dedication – Tony and Linda. Your support and kindness are greatly appreciated.

I never thought I'd write a book, but it has been an interesting experience. I must thank Teresa Daly of Gill Books, who approached me and suggested I tell my story. And in that regard I must also thank Tommy Tiernan, because it was the interview I did on his show that brought me to Teresa's attention.

I think gratitude is a good path to happiness. I'm so grateful for my career and for all the opportunities it presented to me, and for all the people it brought into my life. I have been the recipient of so much positivity and goodwill, and I never underestimate that. Thank you, colleagues, friends and family for bestowing such a wealth of happiness on my life. I truly am grateful.

Contents

PROLOGUE

The youngsters were playing on Mountjoy Square, poking about in the broken-down remains of an old wall that had collapsed. There was rubble and dust everywhere, but to young lads in 1950s Dublin, this was a playground, an explorer's paradise. One of the boys noticed a scrap of yellow. He bent down to examine it and discovered it was hard, metal, and the red words on the side said 'Colman's Mustard'.

He shook it, and something shifted about inside. But it didn't feel like a clogged lump of mustard powder, as he expected. It was looser, and it made a soft slapping sound as it hit the lid and then the base. The boy worked at the lid, prising it off with his fingers, eager to get to whatever was inside before his pals came over and ruined it.

The lid finally popped open. He looked inside. It was a rolled-up bundle of cash. Actual banknotes, more than he'd ever seen. There must be hundreds in there. It was a lot of money to lose. Someone had pushed it into the mustard tin to keep it safe. But if everything was rubble, wouldn't that person be long dead? If he kept it, they'd never know. But still...

∽৹∾

In 1959, I was a very young solicitor in my first job outside my uncle's practice, working with Roger Greene & Sons on Wellington Quay in Dublin. I covered food hygiene cases and the like, all very desk-based, methodical and predictable. On this particular day, a young fellow came into the office looking for assistance. The receptionist brought him over to my desk, where I was busy working. He told me his story: the previous year, he had found a large sum of money in a mustard tin over at Mountjoy Square, and he had handed it in to the local garda station. The gardaí had told him that after one year and one day, the money would be his to keep, if it wasn't claimed in that time. A year to the day after the lad had handed it over, an elderly man had turned up at the garda station, claiming that the tin and its valuable stash belonged to his deceased wife, and that he wished to retrieve it. As a result, the young fellow standing before me had been told to attend at the Bridewell Courthouse for an application to be made to the court regarding the money.

Since I had court experience, albeit confined to civil court cases, I was deputed to go with the young fellow and to act as his solicitor. This was highly unusual and took me by surprise. It was rare to see a woman in the criminal courts – on either side of the dock. Women had been able to practise as solicitors and be called to the Bar since 1919, but the hallowed environs of the criminal courts remained notably woman-free. The prevailing opinion was that criminal law was too uncouth for females, so those doors were generally closed to us by implicit consensus. But now here I was, being told to march into the lion's den. It was entirely unexpected. Nonetheless, down we went to the Bridewell, on Chancery Street, a place I had never been to in my life and had never had any wish to go to, either. It was a courthouse for proper crimes and proper criminals, which was nothing to do with me or the work I did.

The Bridewell was a squat but imposing edifice, built of Wicklow granite with railings around it. To me, it looked like a prison block: grey and, frankly, a bit frightening. I hesitated at the entrance, but my young charge was looking to me for guidance, so I pushed back my shoulders, made sure my hat was firmly in place – it was compulsory for women to wear hats in the courthouse, then – and in we walked through the grand doorway.

Inside, it was chaos. There seemed to be vast crowds of people – detectives, gardaí, criminals, legal folks of all sorts. I felt a bit overcome, and I'm sure my companion felt the same way. Thankfully, a solicitor friend of my uncle's – a man on whose knee

I used to sit as a child – came over and proffered his hand. He said to us, 'The money is yours.' It turned out he was acting for the elderly claimant and that his client had changed his mind about the claim. There must have been a story behind his sudden change of heart, but I didn't ask what it was. I simply presumed the claim wasn't bona fide in some way and accepted that it was being dropped. Whatever the reason, the hearing was quick and straightforward as a result, and I never had to open my mouth. God knows what the judge would have thought of a young female solicitor speaking from the brown floor. I was very glad to be spared that. The money, which amounted to £400, was handed over to the honest young man. That was a lot of money at the time. He told me he was going to buy himself a motorbike and all the gear to go with it.

I nearly ran out of the Bridewell afterwards. It was a foreign country to me, and I was itching to cross the border back to the 'normal' world. The crowds, the noise, the labyrinth of rooms… it was all completely alien. I didn't like being in close proximity to what I saw as hardened criminals. And it was very much a man's world, I could see that. There was an edge to the whole experience that felt dangerous, a bit sinister, like anything could happen, and I'd be stuck in the middle of it and no clue what to do.

I was too nervous to take in any distinct impressions of the place and the proceedings, but I was left with one very, very clear thought: *This is not for me.*

I had a lot to learn.

CHAPTER I

IT'S FRIGHTENING HOW EASILY YOU COULD MISS A PATH IN LIFE

I'm a left-hander and an only child, which are two crucial things to know about me. One gave me a strong sense of injustice, the other gave me a strong sense of self-reliance, and somewhere in between the two lies my unexpected career as a District Court judge. That path certainly wasn't written in the stars, but once I'd stumbled on to it, those seemingly innocuous qualities proved invaluable.

I wasn't aware of these things when I was young, of course. Life's patterns only become apparent as you get older. The benefit of living long enough to reach old age is that your perspective widens with the passing years, until you eventually see the inter-connections clearly and discover how many people to whom you owe a debt of gratitude – even if you once considered them to have done you a disservice. I find it almost amusing how very differently I see things now, looking back from the vantage point of 84 years – and counting.

For a long time – most of my life, really – I felt that being an only child was a major disadvantage and an obstacle I had to strive to overcome. I had no vocabulary for so many things because I had no one to talk to, no one with whom to discuss and decipher my life experiences. There was a big gap between me and my parents: I had quite a Victorian, stand-offish upbringing, and that meant there was no space for personal talk or emotions. I felt there was a deep silence inside me and around me, and I couldn't speak my way out of it with anyone. It took decades before I could finally see the benefits of this situation. In fact, it was the solitude of lockdown in 2020 that set me thinking along new lines. I realised then that being an only child had fed directly into the type of judge I became and into my ability to manage a District Court, where you have no jury to play a role in your decision-making. I had to trust my own instincts and judgement in all matters. Now I realised that it came easily to me because I had, in fact, been doing it all my life. My lack of siblings and the tenor of my upbringing had most certainly moulded my personality. I had always assumed they had moulded it poorly, but actually they had moulded it to fit my eventual path in life. It was a pattern it took me a lifetime to appreciate.

Not only was I an only child, I was a left-handed only child at that – curses upon curses. This 'disability' caused great consternation, in particular to my father, who believed it was a matter of choice and that I simply had to decide to be right-handed. I think he felt it was a mark of contrariness that my left hand shot out to do things of its own accord, robbing my right hand of its rightful dominance. I remember a day on Killiney Beach, skimming stones with my father and a school friend of mine. Without thinking, I was skimming them beautifully with my left hand. My father became irritated. 'No, no, no,' he insisted, 'you do that with your right hand.' I took the next stone into my right hand and tried my best to obey him. I launched the stone, and it whizzed off to the side, hitting a man in a boat! My father was still not convinced.

Many people will have this same story to tell from their childhood in 1940s and '50s Ireland. The majority of people were right-handers, and that was seen as the 'correct' way to be. At school, we left-handers were smacked for using our left hands and forced to write with our right hands. Eventually, I began to believe it myself and I went through school and college as a right-hander, a member of the herd. But when I was in my twenties, I was in a car accident and suffered a whiplash injury, which necessitated consultations with an orthopaedic surgeon. He asked about my dominant side, and I told him I was right-handed. I'd been fully brainwashed by that stage, obviously. That surgeon was so clever. He'd casually hand me something or drop something near my chair, and I'd reach out to take it or pick it up – and I'd always use my left hand. This happened over several visits, until eventually one day he told me I was left-handed and no doubt about it.

That wasn't enough to secure me a happy life as a left-hander, though. My father's influence on me was very strong, and it didn't diminish with age. As late as 1975, when my eldest son made his Confirmation, my father bought a small snooker table as a gift for him, and we all gathered around to play. I took the cue in my left hand, and my father immediately said, 'No, you don't play this game with the left hand.' I put down the cue, coldly announced the end of my snooker career and walked away from the table. For years I didn't play, even though I loved the game. But much later – after my mother had died, and my father was living with me and the children – we watched Jimmy White play in his left-handed glory, and my father didn't say he shouldn't be playing like that. My father then bought a full-sized table, and it became our nightly ritual, whenever I was at home, to play three or four frames together – and I played them all with my left hand. My father remained convinced that I ought to be right-handed, but he stopped remarking on it during those regular games. We did that until a week before his death at 90 years of age, in 1996.

This seemingly minor issue has bothered me all my life. I resent that I was forced to conform, to go against my own natural inclination and to adhere to a notion of what was 'correct'. To this day, it annoys me that I was subjected to that. I think, looking back, this was where my own sense of injustice came from, and it was what allowed me to work towards understanding those accused of crimes as much as those who were victims of crimes. That ability doesn't come easily to everyone – moving from the victim's point of view to the accused's point of view takes some doing – but having experienced that treatment from my early years primed me to look into the *why* of what people did, not just at the act itself. In time, that came to define my whole approach to hearing cases and passing judgments on them. It gave me a very strong sense that people are individuals and cannot be lumped together – that is unfair, and it nearly always obscures the truth of the matter. It sounds odd that this flowed from being discriminated against for being a left-hander, but there you go – our motivations can come from the strangest sources.

Another source of injustice was the nun who regularly rapped my knuckles during piano practice. I took up playing at the age of six and progressed quickly, but that didn't save me from having a ruler slapped against my knuckles with grim regularity. The idea of beating anything into children is abhorrent to me. It achieves nothing other than to foster bitter resentment. Thankfully, she didn't ruin my love of music, which was a miracle in itself. And I learned that negative experiences can be the basis for very positive outcomes. When I attended the Royal Irish Academy of Music as a teenager, playing piano and cello, the kind and encouraging tuition I received there stood in stark contrast to the nunnish lessons I had been used to. As a result, I was able to take huge joy in this new approach to music, all the more so because I was coming from a place of joyless repetition. I thrived in these surroundings and decided that I would go on to study music in college. My life plan was a degree in music, a BMus, followed by recitals, concerts and perhaps teaching later on. I was eager to live it.

Then, I fell ill. I was ill enough that my mother called the doctor to visit me at home. As he examined me and wrote out a prescription, he chatted to my mother about my future plans. She told him that I was preparing to study music at college. The doctor raised an eyebrow and said emphatically, 'There's no money in that. Do law.' It's hard to explain why, but we obeyed him. My mother shared his opinion with my father, and the doctor's authoritative words took precedence over any of mine, and that was that. Suddenly, I was headed for a law degree instead of a life in music. I'm sure that will sound extremely odd to the young people of today, but at that time, as a young person with a strict father, you felt you didn't have any choices. We were instructed by our parents, and we heeded those instructions, usually to the letter. This was no different. My father had spoken, and I put aside my lovely plan for my future and got on with it.

In a way, though, it made sense, because my father had often told me that I wasn't a creative person, that I didn't have a creative mind. Whenever I had to write a fictional story for school, it would inevitably end in tears and with him saying, 'Open your mind, you bloody little fool.' Those were the only times I ever heard him use such language, and it was shocking to me. But that idea, that I was incapable of creativity, stuck fast. I'm not sure if the idea held on to me or if I held on to it, but in my mind it became an absolute rule that I believed defined my character. If I wasn't in any way creative, then perhaps a life in law would suit me best, even if I didn't want to do it. I think there was some sort of reasoning of that kind going on beneath the surface to allow me to be sweetly obedient on the matter. It is only in writing this book and looking back over my life and career for the first time, that I have come to understand that my father was not entirely correct in his assessment of me. He was very harsh. But it amazes me just how long it takes to gain that sort of insight when a label has been affixed to you in childhood – it's both astonishing and upsetting.

So off I went to law school at University College Dublin (UCD) and at the Incorporated Law Society, which was then situated in a section of the Four Courts building. There were just two other women in my whole year. I had to bat off constant comments about entering a 'man's profession', as if there were something inherently wrong with me because I was studying a 'man's subject'. I knew I wasn't on level pegging with the male students, but there was no outright hostility. I didn't dwell on this attitude at the time. I was perfectly capable of what the course demanded, and that's all that mattered to me. I didn't have the first idea what being a solicitor would entail, but after four years' study I did at least have a decent grasp of the many different elements of Irish law. I didn't see it at the time, but I think it was to my advantage that I had no sense of entitlement about my studies. So many of my fellow male students were following a line already drawn by their fathers and grandfathers, along a path that was preordained for them. It gave them a sense of entitlement, but likely also one of entrapment. I didn't have that. Yes, I had the choice made for me by my parents, but I wasn't burdened with the same sense of having to fulfil a family obligation. I think that gave me a unique attitude, which was certainly clear when I was on the bench and working alongside male judges, who by and large took a markedly different approach from me.

The biggest influence on my working life, though, was undoubtedly my uncle, Anthony

Hussey. He acted as my master throughout my studies, starting in September 1954, and he took his role very seriously. His practice was an average-sized one, located on Leinster Street South, near the back entrance to Trinity College. It was upstairs, over a manufacturing premises. In addition to my uncle and Michael O'Higgins TD, the two partners, there were two secretaries and two apprentices – me and a chap apprenticed to Mr O'Higgins. Every student had to sign up to a master, but from what I could see, they rarely had any truck with them. The other students went for coffee after lectures and generally gadded about, but I was worked very hard by my uncle. At the time, I didn't like his strictness, but I'm so grateful to him and I respect him so much for all he taught me. He knew I was going out into a man's world, that I would face prejudice and often be the only woman in the courtroom, and he wanted me to be ready to face that. I was young and female, and he was very aware of how that would translate in the workplace. He had once sent me to a cattle mart to get a dealer to sign a particular document, and I was promptly put into the ring and 'sold'. I took it as a joke and laughed, but my uncle saw it in a far more sober light. Therefore, he insisted that I be a perfectionist in everything I did and ensured I had a solid grounding in the various offices with which a solicitor must interact.

I continued to work with my uncle after I graduated, but in 1959 it was time for a change, so I applied for a job with Roger Greene & Sons. I had decent civil court experience under my belt by then, and I was a good candidate for the position. At the interview, I got on very well with Mr Denis Greene, who had run the practice on his own since the death of his brother, Roger, and I think he could see that I was well drilled and competent. He offered me the job, at a salary of ten pounds a week. My uncle was paying me six guineas a week (slightly over six pounds today). I was taken aback by this largesse. In fact, a sort of fear surged through me at being deemed good enough to warrant such a pay rise. I said to Mr Greene, 'I don't think I'm worth it. I can't accept ten pounds.' If he was surprised by this self-assessment, he didn't show it. We shook on eight pounds, and I became a solicitor at his firm. Two weeks later, Mr Greene acknowledged that he was very impressed with my work, and more importantly, I had proven myself to myself, so I belatedly accepted the original offer of ten pounds a week.

Denis Greene was a very caring man and a wonderful mentor. I can still see him poring over every single legal letter we wrote, checking carefully and making corrections. He always urged us not to say too much, not to repeat and never over-explain. That was a valuable lesson. Whenever I had a person in the dock who spoke on and on, repeating, looping back, rephrasing the same statement in multiple different ways, beset by nerves and the desperate desire to be believed, I would think of Denis Greene and his common sense. When we say too much, we usually say too much. It's best to stick with the substance of the matter, I have found.

I left Greene & Sons in 1961, when I got married. That was before the days of working mothers being the norm. Most men, and I can include my husband among them, disliked the notion of their wife being divided between private life and public life. Everything ran more smoothly if the woman gave up her own ambitions and interests and subsumed herself into household work and child-rearing – and supporting her husband's ambitions and interests.

That was regarded as the proper order, upheld by the Constitution itself, which stated that 'mothers shall not be obliged by economic necessity to engage in labour to the neglect of their duties in the home'. It was a powerful argument for any husband to have in his back pocket – you were *supposed* to put your home duties first. For the majority of women, that was their lived reality, and to be honest, many questioned it as little as their husbands did.

And so, the next 10 years were taken up with starting a family and running a household with three children. There is much about housewifery that is deadly boring, especially for a young woman who had been independent and running about in the world, but once again I fell in with what was expected of me. However, that all changed when my marriage ended unexpectedly in October 1972. This wasn't part of the plan at all – it wasn't part of anyone's plan in those days. I was a single mother with three children at a time when single mothers were largely vilified. I was lucky, of course, in that I had financial help from my parents and my ex-husband, so we weren't hard up, but it was a very challenging time regardless. In 1973, I decided

I had to return to work, for everyone's sake. I was miserable being chained to the house all day, and I was all too aware of the nice women of my neighbourhood, who drank at all hours of the day in what was a graceful swoop into genteel alcoholism. Those women often confessed to me that they were bored beyond measure but felt there was no alternative, and I was terrified of becoming one of them. I went back to work as a solicitor – just part-time, so I could be a mother too, but it was a lifesaver.

Over the next decade, between 1973 and 1982, I worked part-time in three different law firms. The notion of part-time legal work was a very recent innovation at the time, no doubt in response to the numbers of women starting to come through with law degrees, and it suited me down to the ground. If that hadn't been the case, I wouldn't have been able to combine work and home and school, so I was incredibly grateful that the legal world had moved on in that regard and could facilitate my need for reduced daily working hours. The profession was still very male-dominated, but more and more women were pursuing a career in the law, so I was no longer quite so isolated as I had been in my college days. As a solicitor, I was given court work, civil cases, that sort of thing. I was once tasked with attending the Bridewell – for that money-in-a-tin case – but it was almost unheard of for women to work in the criminal courts. We were a sheltered bunch back then, regarded as too delicate to be subjected to the raw details of crime cases. And I didn't mind, because the criminal side terrified me. I had no sense that I belonged there.

After 10 years, my children were near or beyond 18 years of age, and my future was looking a bit less hectic. As an innately independent person, I had no interest in meeting a new partner or sharing my home and life with a man. I very much enjoyed my own set-up and the freedom it afforded me. And now, with the children beginning to leave the roost, my time was becoming my own again. So, in the way of these unpredictable life patterns, when I bumped into a fellow solicitor in 1984 and he told me they were looking for female candidates for the District Court bench, I was in a good position to listen. He told me that a woman district justice had resigned, and another female candidate was being sought to replace her. While the higher courts, at that time, remained open only to barristers, solicitors could apply for the District Court bench. My first reaction was the same as with Mr Greene: *I'm not good enough, I couldn't possibly become a judge.* But I found myself thinking about it constantly, nonetheless. I had never in my life seen myself as judge material, but for some reason I felt compelled to try. My decision was bolstered by the support of my children, who thought it was a good idea. I had never needed a CV before in my life and hadn't a clue how to prepare one, so I asked a young solicitor friend to write it up for me, and I posted it off.

I must be honest about my path to the bench and the success of that application. In those days, it was still very much a case of who you knew, and the old boys' network was robust. The reason they were seeking a female applicant was that there was a female judge to be replaced. It turned out that a woman had been appointed to the bench a few months prior to this. She was a married woman with her own firm, and the additional work of being a court judge proved simply too much for her to juggle, so she resigned. That left a vacancy for a suitable female candidate. Was I a suitable candidate? Well,

I had extensive court experience as a solicitor, and I was conscientious and hardworking, so on paper it looked a good fit. But even then, I too benefited from the 'who you know' system.

My cousin was married to Gemma Hussey, who was Minister for Education in 1984. I received a phone call from Gemma one day, and she told me that my application was being looked upon favourably. However, she went on, the government didn't want egg on its face, so it was necessary to ask if I was planning to take my ex-husband to court for maintenance. I replied that my marriage had ended 12 years previously and was now water under the bridge, so there would certainly be no proceedings. It was irritating to be asked, but I understood the concern to avoid a public and unseemly court case and any unwelcome, sneering headlines it might generate. This entire concern rested on the fact that I was a woman – of that I'm sure. Appointing a female judge was daring enough in the early 1980s, but if a private controversy of that nature had been added to the mix, it would have unleashed very strong opinions about the role of women in the legal profes-sions. If I had become the story in such a manner, it would have maligned and undermined all of my female colleagues. This was the 1984 mindset, you must remember. I knew what I was being asked, and why, and I put their fears to rest as resolutely as I could – even though I felt no male colleague in my position would have been asked the same question.

It wasn't long after that phone call that I received the news that my application had been accepted. I don't think I would have been chosen if it wasn't for the Hussey surname and that quiet confirmation that I wouldn't cause any embarrassment with my separated, single-parent status. A slightly bitter pill to swallow at the time, but I'm glad I did. I wish I could say it was entirely merit-based, but the fact is that it wasn't – not for me and not for anyone else.

I had to readjust my thinking to get my head around the idea of me being a judge in the District Court. It wasn't planned, it felt entirely accidental, but now I had to show up and play the role convincingly. There was no training for judges at that time: you were simply handed the job and you had to go and do it. That was extremely daunting. I knew I had so much to learn, but I also knew that I would have to learn it on the job.

The District Court would be my home, a court of limited jurisdiction hearing cases of civil law, family law and criminal law. There is no jury at district level, so only those offences classed as minor criminal offences could be heard there. For all other criminal offences, the District Court served as an entranceway to the higher courts system, remanding those in custody or on bail and sending their cases forward to the appropriate court.

The Irish court system wasn't that old when I joined – it was only after Independence in 1921 that Ireland had its own legislature, separate from Britain. The Constitution (Bunreacht na hÉireann) was ratified in 1937 and became the fundamental law of the Irish State. It established the court system, which comprises:

- the District Court;
- the Circuit Court, which sits with or without a jury depending on the case, is also of limited jurisdiction and also hears family, civil and criminal cases, but with a higher threshold in each – for example, it can deal with claims above €15,000, which is the limit of the District Court, and up to €75,000 (those are the current thresholds – they

were, of course, far lower figures in my day, but the same demarcation of thresholds applied); it can also grant orders of divorce;

- the High Court/Central Criminal Court, which has full jurisdiction on civil and criminal matters, which means it hears cases of the most serious criminal offences. This court can be judge(s)-only or judge and jury, but when acting as the Central Criminal Court a 12-person jury serves alongside the judge;

- the Special Criminal Court, which has no jury and is presided over by three judges who hear scheduled offences, classed as 'subversive crimes' and crimes against the state, and those cases that the Office of the Director of Public Prosecutions (DPP) deems to require special circumstances in order for justice to be served, such as where there is a concern that jury members might be subject to intimidation or coercion;

- the Court of Appeal, which again has no jury and is presided over by three judges who hear appeals based on constitutional law, civil law and criminal law deriving from the Circuit Court, Central Criminal Court and Special Criminal Court, and also cases stated from the Circuit and High courts, which is an option available to judges who require interpretation of a point of law in order to proceed with a judgment; and finally

- the top tier: the Supreme Court, which is the court of final appeal in Ireland.

Each court has a president who oversees the workings of that court tier nationwide, while the Supreme Court is the preserve of the Chief Justice of Ireland. And, of course, the whole court system has been fed by the DPP since its establishment in 1974, when it took over the role of state prosecution service from the Attorney General.

It is an interlinked, hardworking system, and its foundation stone is the district level, which processes the vast majority of crimes and criminals. As such, the District Court is the largest entity in the criminal justice system, with regional courts nationwide and several courts in the larger cities, like Dublin and Cork, each with its own bailiwick, or jurisdiction. There are currently about 64 District Court judges, which is far more than any other court – naturally enough, given there are 23 district courts nationwide and then the Dublin Metropolitan Area on top of that. Each court has a permanent judge or judges, as well as moveable judges who go to where they are needed. So I was joining a large cohort of colleagues with a large and largely unpredictable caseload that covered a fairly wide range of applicable law. However, I would be joining the District Court of the Dublin Metropolitan Area, which has a different set-up. For the populous area of Dublin, the various strands of the District Court's proceedings – civil, family, criminal, summonses, licensing and others – are divided among different courthouses and courtrooms. That meant I would be assigned to a particular area of the law, which, I reassured myself, would make it easier to navigate.

All judges are sworn in at a special ceremony during which they take an oath as set out in Article 34.6.1 of the Constitution, affirming that they will enact their duties independently, 'subject only to this Constitution and the law'. In my day, it was a formal ceremony held in the Supreme Court with the Chief Justice presiding, if possible, or a Supreme Court judge. The ceremony for judges being sworn in to the higher courts was held in Áras an Uachtaráin in the Phoenix Park – another example of how the District Court judges were treated differently. For my ceremony, I wore a smart suit and my judge's gown, which somewhat helped overcome the imposter syndrome I was feeling. My father and three children were there to witness this historic moment in my life. It was a very short ceremony, during which I took my oath with my hand on the Bible. I was sworn in with two male judges of the District Court, and I was appointed a temporary justice, rather than being assigned to a particular district. It was all over very quickly, and there I stood: Temporary Justice Gillian Hussey.

About 18 months after my original oath-taking, I went through a second swearing-in ceremony when I was formally appointed to the Dublin Metropolitan District as a permanent district justice. On that occasion, a male colleague was being sworn in for the first time as a temporary justice – taking my place under that particular title. Some time after that, a District Court justice in the West of Ireland took a case to the High Court to challenge the titles we used. At that time, the judges at District Court level were called justices. This echoed the title 'justice of the peace', which was a political appointment separate to the judiciary. That was why this particular judge argued that all judges should be called judges, and that the justice label should be consigned to the bin. Personally, I didn't care what I was called, but evidently some people felt very strongly about it. The case was heard in the High Court, and my colleague won. From then on, we were no longer 'justice' or 'temporary' – we were simply District Court judges. They didn't bother with a new ceremony for all of us that time. The name was handed down from on high, and that was that – equality at last!

When I donned my black gown, I was following in the footsteps of many women in the legal profession, although not many female judges. Women had been admitted to practice law since 1919, thanks to the Sex Disqualification (Removal) Act, and there had been a steady stream of female barristers and solicitors since then. In 1921 Averil Deverell and Frances Kyle were called to the Bar on the same day, becoming the first female barristers in Ireland and Britain, while the first solicitor was Mary Dorothea Heron in 1923. But it took much longer for women to ascend to the judge's chair. The first woman to do so was Eileen Kennedy, who was appointed to the District Court in 1964, 20 years before me. But progress was very slow. It wasn't until 1980 that Mella Carroll became the first High Court judge. I always liked the story that Mella Carroll was referred to as 'My Lord' for the first decade of her tenure, until she requested that she be addressed as 'Judge' in future. The first female Supreme Court judge was Susan Denham (now Ireland's first female Chief Justice) in 1992, and the Circuit Court followed suit in 1993 when Catherine McGuinness was appointed to its ranks. And it took even longer, until 2011, for the first female DPP, a role held by Claire Loftus until 2021. So while the District Court had been first established in 1924, it took 40 years for its first female judge to take up residence, and the rest of us came dropping slow after that. It was a century of change, but it took time for that change to reach the higher echelons. There was precedent for me in terms of graduating as a female solicitor, even though I was one of only three women in my year, but when I took the oath to become a District Court judge, it felt far more like taking part in slowly forging a new path. I didn't have so many women to follow into that room, so I knew I would have to make my own way for the most part. However, that suited me very well, with my only child's natural sense of self-reliance and separateness.

After I was sworn in, my first posting was to Dolphin House Court, which dealt with family law and civil litigation and was therefore seen as a natural fit for a female judge. This was largely the area I was used to being involved in, so I managed quite well – with the help of the wonderful registrars who ran the court so efficiently. I was judge and jury, and that also suited me well. I wasn't afraid of relying on my own instincts. I think it was also important and helpful that I came to the bench when I was 47 years old. I had the benefit of age and the ability to see life's grey areas – and understand them. I also feel that my age meant I had more empathy with those in the courtroom, and I mean with everyone – the victim, the accused, the gardaí and the family members who dragged on endless cigarettes out in the hallways, nursing their heavy silences under a pall of smoke. I was more open to the plethora of experiences being described and very willing to listen and learn. I was also aware that being single was a huge advantage: I was able to devote almost all of my time to my work because I was free to do so – the children were fine and quite grown, my father was living with us then, so I had that additional backup, and everyone was secure and relatively happy. I had the freedom to commit to my job, and I did so to the extent that it became a way of life. It all meshed perfectly because the timing was right and the circumstances were right – even if those circumstances had once seemed all wrong.

I was only seven weeks on the bench in Dolphin House when a case came before me that was a cause célèbre – just my luck! In May 1984, the Well Woman Centre (WWC) was charged with selling contraceptives contrary to the Health (Family Planning) Act 1979. As a judge, you don't know the cases coming before you in advance, so you can't read up or otherwise make specific preparations for a hearing. You must go by your own knowledge and the information being laid out before you by the defence and the prosecution. In this case, the barrister for the state was Gerry Danaher, and he set out the case that the WWC had broken the law by selling condoms. This was at a time of huge change and controversy in Ireland around the whole area of reproductive rights and women's rights. At the start of that year, a young girl called Ann Lovett had died in a grotto in County Longford while giving birth to a baby no one knew about. It was a deeply tragic case, and it highlighted the consequences of intolerant attitudes to sex and pregnancy. This was before people were made aware of the true workings of the mother and baby homes, but there was a rising sense of anger, and some sections of society were increasingly vocal about the desperate need for change. The WWC was an advocate for reproductive rights and women's right to choose, hence its decision to sell contraceptives. Now I had to decide if the Centre had done so illegally and therefore should be prosecuted.

The day of the hearing, the court was full to capacity. I was taken aback when I walked through the doors and was confronted by a sea of people. I was even more taken aback when my cousin Barbara, a solicitor, walked in, with her barrister, and prepared to represent the WWC case. Neither of us had any idea the other was involved until that moment. It was embarrassing, but we soldiered on. A packet of condoms was handed up to my bench as evidence, and the two sides proceeded to deliver their arguments. After listening to all the information, I realised that the District Court couldn't decide this matter without some legal clarifications. I therefore stated the case to the High Court, seeking answers to a number of points of law. Unfortunately, that meant the big day out ended without a climax, as I adjourned the case until a document setting out the facts and the questions requiring clarification was prepared and submitted to the High Court, and then returned to the District Court. As I stood up to leave the bench, Gerry Danaher, who was a tall, whimsical man with a sense of devilment, asked politely, 'Will you be needing those, Judge?' It was normal procedure to return items of evidence, but I was too new to know that. He gave me a great laugh with that mischievous comment.

The case was eventually tried in the High Court and then in the Supreme Court, before finally ending up in the European Court of Justice (ECJ). None of that had anything to do with me, but I watched its progress with interest. My cousin

Barbara recently told me that the run of appeals was necessary to reach the ECJ, which was the ultimate aim all along. There, the WWC won its case, and there was no prosecution for the sale of condoms. It was a certain indication that major changes were afoot in Ireland, albeit they were arriving slowly and encountering much resistance. But the eventual success of the WWC in this matter was a hopeful sign, I felt.

After six months on the bench between Dolphin House and District Courts 1, 2 and 3, I felt I was somewhat getting the hang of being a District Court judge. I wasn't queasy on the commute to work anymore. I felt more in control, more capable of running the court and making good decisions. I was learning quickly, devoted as I was to the job. Then, everything changed. The lovely president of the District Court at that time was Tommy Donnelly. He ruled with a rod of iron and endeavoured never to let anyone see his soft side, but we all knew it was there. He called me to his office to review my position. I was quite happy in the courts that I had sat in thus far and hoped he was planning to leave me there. However, he told me that he was pleased

LESSONS FROM THE BENCH

with my work so far and was moving me to a new posting: the Bridewell District Court.

I couldn't respond, I was in that much shock. I remembered the Bridewell from my one and only outing there: I couldn't recall seeing a single woman there that day, and I had run from the place gladly. Women weren't sent to the criminal bench of the district courts. What was he thinking? In fact, I think I was the third female judge appointed there, but I didn't know that then, and the very last words I expected to come out of Tommy's mouth were 'the Bridewell'. To me, it was a male preserve, hearing serious cases and based on criminal law, in which I was not particularly well versed, given that we had had only one module on it in college. It was an audacious decision that could have backfired spectacularly on both of us. When word filtered out along the legal grapevine, I'm sure many in the court system were surprised at the prospect of this newly minted female judge being sent to sit at the Bridewell.

I couldn't refuse the posting – that was not the done thing – but I was absolutely petrified at the prospect of it. It felt surreal, in fact. I had ended up doing law unexpectedly, my marriage had ended unexpectedly, I had applied for a court position unexpectedly and now, most unexpectedly of all, I was being sent to the criminal bench at the Bridewell District Court. It seemed a huge mistake. A ridiculous, horrible mistake. But it wasn't a mistake at all. As it turned out, it was to be the central motif of my life's pattern. I'm so grateful that I didn't miss that unexpected path. Tommy Donnelly's incredible decision was not just life-changing – it was life-defining.

CHAPTER 2

YOU WILL MAKE MISTAKES AS YOU LEARN, AND YOU MUST APOLOGISE FOR THEM

The Bridewell District Court was like a madhouse, and I lost half a stone in my first few weeks working there. On my first day, I was in a state of terror, barely able to think straight and take everything in. I didn't know where the dock was, I didn't know where I was to sit, I didn't know the solicitors or the detectives or the uniformed gardaí. There was no induction day or training to get me up to speed. I just arrived at Chancery Street, walked through those doors and that was it – Judge Gillian Hussey was officially on duty. Perish the thought!

Inside the building, it was quite overwhelming – just as it had been on my first visit all those years ago. There were detectives swarming everywhere, criminals loitering, some in handcuffs, and a dense scrum of legal types, all laden with files and folders and dashing about as if the place was on fire. Mostly, I couldn't tell the criminals from the gardaí. The residents of the vicinity treated the Bridewell as a sort of local theatre, a place they came to each day for entertainment and warmth, adding to the melee of bodies and voices. It felt utterly chaotic, so many comings and goings, so much noise, such a dense fog of cigarette smoke in the passageway. The whole effect was desperately intimidating.

My only friend in all this chaos was my registrar, Alberta Egan, who introduced herself to me and helped me get settled. My gratitude to her knew no bounds – I am still expressing it to this day as we remain friends. She gave me a quick debriefing on the normal run of things before the day got under way. As registrar, it was her job to organise the schedule of hearings for the day, to handle the charge sheets and all the paperwork, to announce which case was up next and to liaise with the gardaí and detectives involved in each case. Basically, it was up to her to ensure the court ran smoothly. The normal running order was remand cases and pleas in the mornings, and then, in the afternoon, hearings for those who had entered pleas of not guilty. It was an onerous task but, like all of the registrars I ever worked with, Alberta performed it with calm and remarkable efficiency.

It is a strange feeling to sit down into your judge's chair, which is usually situated at a height above everyone else in court, and to know that you and you alone must listen to, assess and pass judgment on whatever comes before you – and, of course, you never know what is going to be brought before you. It was not lonely, as such – I was so independent that thought simply wouldn't have occurred to me – but it was a huge responsibility, and I felt that very keenly every day of my 17 years on the criminal bench. I owed it to everyone present to conduct myself appropriately and do a good job. This was life and liberty stuff, and that could never be taken lightly. So on that first day in the Bridewell, I was focused on breathing – which was suddenly a bit of a challenge – and on listening and learning. As it happened, that would turn out to be how I spent every minute in that chair.

When the first case was called, there was a shuffling sound beneath my feet that grew louder and louder. Footsteps. And then, suddenly, a head emerged from the floor. I worked to hide my surprise as another head popped up and proceeded to enter the courtroom. I had no idea that the cells were below the court and that prisoners were escorted up the stairs and into the room itself though an opening in the floor. I also didn't know that emerging from that particular spot meant the person was in custody. I didn't know what was going on down there at all! So that's how the day started, with a sudden appearance and a mental note to find out where they had ascended from. Then, we were off.

The District Court is not at the glamorous end of the law. It is a processing house that is open to all comers. There are certain crimes that immediately bypass the District Court for the higher courts – such as those eligible to be heard in the Special Criminal Court – but most people accused of a crime enter

LESSONS FROM THE BENCH

the judicial system via a charge in the District Court. When a person is so charged, the case is remanded. This allows the DPP, in certain cases, to decide in which court the case ought to be heard. In theory, a District Court judge can disagree with the DPP's designation. I respected the work of the DPP. If the case is going forward to a higher court, a Book of Evidence must be prepared by An Garda. If the case is to remain in the District Court, a date is set for the hearing. All of this translates into long and hectic days – and you have those every day. It is a vastly busy court system, taking care of the whole gamut of criminal actions, from the petty to the serious. It was fast and furious, and I had to be mentally alert at all times. This was all markedly different from what I was used to in the civil courts, but I soon found it was utterly compelling. I might have been way beyond my comfort zone, but I discovered that it was quite a thrilling place to experience.

The Bridewell's Court 6 bailiwick included Ballymun, Finglas and Coolock, all on Dublin city's Northside. These were areas of Dublin with which I wasn't familiar, with social problems and levels of poverty that differed markedly from the place where I had grown up and gone to school. It was utterly eye-opening for me to meet the people from these areas in the court and hear about their lives and challenges. It quickly became apparent that many of the crimes that came before me could be described as 'survival crimes': acts of theft and the like committed by people who had very little and few opportunities to improve their lot. These were the forgotten communities, the ones who would be left behind as Ireland roared towards the Celtic Tiger years. I was largely ignorant of the abuse of alcohol and drugs, but here it was a constant presence, shadowing those in the dock, often for the whole of their lives, thanks to their parents' addictions. It was quite humbling to realise that my own quietly ordered life was, in fact, a paradise of privilege, and that I had been spared the bad luck and unfavourable environments of those who stood before me simply by the circumstances of my birth. I was on an extremely steep learning curve in every way from day one, that's for sure.

There were very few ways to educate myself on the work I was expected to do, but one of those ways was lunch with my fellow District Court judges in the Bridewell. This formal occasion was observed daily, with the president of the District Court taking his place at the head of the table. No one else would dare lower their posterior on to that dining chair – it was an unspoken and unbroken rule. Once gathered together, we would discuss cases and judgments – although I tended to do an awful lot of listening as I strove to learn quickly what I needed to know to execute my task well. It wasn't all good advice, though. I remember an older judge at the table who retired from the Bridewell three weeks after I started. Recently, I saw a documentary that featured him and the case of drug dealer Larry Dunne, who was brought before him charged with drug possession. Dunne wasn't convicted, and he cheekily requested his personal items – the drugs, in other words – be returned to him by An Garda. The judge granted his request. I was flabbergasted when I saw it – and it was that same judge who held court at lunch in the Bridewell. However, I understand that judge was by far the most spot on, usually.

I wasn't really a joiner, but I did my best to be attentive and polite with my colleagues. However, I soon learned that they had given me a nickname behind my back: Reverend Mother. It was intended as an insult, but I can't say I cared – after all, that nickname wasn't as bad as the other one I was told about. I got that one courtesy of a female judge who seemed to hate me on sight and who, it seems, only ever referred to me as 'that bitch Hussey'. I don't know what irked this judge about me, and I wasn't inclined to give it the time of day. Whatever it was, it was her problem, not mine. This same judge rang me once, in August 1984, several months after my appointment. A contact of this sort from the particular judge was an unprecedented occurrence. My father took the message, which was to return the call. When I did, the judge snidely informed me that it was being said in the Law Library that I had 'kept the condoms', a reference to the Well Woman Centre case. Innuendoes galore in the sotto voce delivery. I listened to this nonsense then replied, 'That's odd, seeing as the Law Library is closed.' Needless to say, we never became friends.

I had started out with good intentions, but these childish incidents meant I was glad to just get on with my job. There were judges' conferences twice a year, one in Dublin and one at a rural venue outside Dublin. I went along to the first one, open to learning, but it was a waste of time. There was little relevant discussion that I could attach myself to. I got the impression that it was more of a day out among chums. It quickly got to the stage where I was first in to ask for the Saturday sitting in the Bridewell so I could avoid the conferences held outside Dublin. I had nothing in common with my colleagues other than a job title, and, as ever, I was happy to plough my own furrow.

There are certain things I find difficult to talk about, even now, and one of those is another very pertinent reason for avoiding those conferences. During my second swearing-in ceremony, I was being formalised alongside a judge I greatly admired and respected, Judge William Hamill. We chatted about work and other things, before and after the ceremony, and I remember saying to him that I wasn't enamoured with some of his male colleagues. I told him that certain men among his ilk saw women as playthings – even in the professional sphere. He was astounded by this revelation and simply couldn't believe his fellow judges could act in such manner. However, I was telling the truth as it was for me and other female judges.

We didn't tend to talk about such things, but I did go to one conference early on in the company of Justice Mary Kotsonouris, who had suggested we attend together – a safety-in-numbers approach. Although we went to the conference dinner together, we were not seated at the same table. I was seated next to a male judge who was, unfortunately, one of the type I had complained about to my friend Judge Hamill. All throughout dinner, this man engaged in unwanted touching. I parried his advances with the minimum of fuss and certainly without confrontation. At the end of the evening, Judge Hamill approached and said quietly, 'I believe you now.' He had seen with his own eyes what a minority of his colleagues got up to when there was a woman present.

The problem was that there were so few women in the room, we stood out. We were wildly outnumbered, and we were easy targets. That was particularly the case at that time, when women were expected to be demure and ladylike and not assert themselves. Woe betide you if you made a fuss – that was simply not the done thing. And I acquiesced in this, in that I didn't tackle this man's behaviour or order him to stop. I dealt with it by ignoring it, physically and mentally. The only answer I could see was to remove myself so that it couldn't happen. And that's what I did. I never went to another of those dinners again, and I know I wasn't the only woman in the legal profession to avoid social occasions like that because of what we might be subjected to by our male colleagues.

It was, of course, only certain judges who behaved in this way. I liked and respected many of my male colleagues, and they would never have dreamed of treating any colleague in this manner. But those men who did see women as playthings had a disproportionate effect, causing many of us to miss out on social and networking opportunities. I have to say, though, those were the only times it happened, at such functions. It never happened with the gardaí, probation officers or court staff – only with certain judges. That's why it heartens me to see women now becoming aware of their right to speak up, their right not to consent and their right to tell a man, in no uncertain terms, to remove his hands from their person. I came from a generation of middle-class women who didn't feel able to do that, and it was to our cost.

In the workplace, in my courtroom, such unpleasantness didn't occur. There, at least, it was an equal pitch, and I was treated with respect. Well, most of the time – a defendant might hurl abuse on a bad day. In those early days of my career, some of the men who would go on to become Ireland's most notorious criminals were brought before me. But they were in the very early days of their careers too, so it was usually for minor charges. They didn't present as the bleak future of crime in the country, but they were certainly headed for bigger things. One of the very first cases I heard involved John Gilligan, who would go on to become a major drug smuggler with links to the murder of the journalist Veronica Guerin. Two detectives had witnessed Gilligan taking 250 videotapes from the back of his HiAce van, which was found to be neither taxed nor insured, and they had seized the tapes. Now, he wanted them back. I watched Gilligan and found him to be a strange little man, constantly shrugging his shoulders, like a nervous tic. He was boastful, although relatively respectful of the court. This was a police property application, of which the only prior knowledge I had was way back in 1959, with the Colman's Mustard tin case. I had no idea whatsoever of the identity of the man before me. I asked him if he was a working man, and he proudly stated that he had never worked a day in his life. That perplexed me. How could that be? Gilligan and his world were totally outside my sphere of knowledge and experience. I decided that if he did not work, it was probable that he did not own the tapes, therefore I refused the application and did not return the tapes to him.

Some months after our initial encounter, I met John Gilligan again in court, this time at a posting in Court 1 in Morgan Place. The Morgan Place Court was located at the back of the Four Courts and heard depositions. These aren't done anymore because they are devilishly time-consuming, which often worked in the defendant's favour. Depositions involved witnesses being called to give evidence, which was written down word for word by the registrar and then signed by the witness – even though there was already a witness statement in the Book of Evidence. On this occasion, Gilligan was charged with stealing washing machines and receiving stolen goods. I admit that I made a mistake on that occasion. I didn't know that I should send forward all of the charges. I thought he could only be charged with either stealing or receiving. As a result, I sent him forward on one charge only, for which he received a much shorter sentence than the gardaí were hoping to secure for him; he only got eighteen months. That was down to my lack of knowledge of the man and of the law. It was not a good day on the bench for me, and I was so annoyed at myself when I realised my error. Later, I made it my business to seek out the detective leading that case, DI Felix McKenna, and apologise to him in person. Unfortunately, that wouldn't be my last such apology.

In the Bridewell, I also encountered Gerry Hutch, who would go on to become known as The Monk. He was later suspected to have carried out one of the biggest robberies in Ireland's history: of the Brinks Allied depot, which netted about £2.8 million for whoever masterminded it. When I met him, though, he was a young man who was in court merely for criminal damage. He struck me as very discreet, an observer who kept a low profile, even when he was right in front of you. I have observed with great interest as the garda pursuit of The Monk has unfolded over the intervening years, culminating in his extradition from Spain to Ireland in 2021 and his imprisonment in connection with a murder charge. It is a testament to the dogged determination of the gardaí to ensure he answered for at least some of his wrongdoings.

The other young criminal who opened my eyes to the burgeoning drugs scene in Dublin, something that had been completely invisible to me up to that point, was Tony Felloni, who would come to be known as King Scum. He was in the dock in the Bridewell on a drugs charge. At that point, the gardaí knew him as a dealer around the Store Street area. The main thing I remember about him is that he was married to a woman called Anne Flynn, who always wore beautiful suits in court and called him 'Ant-nie' – I heard no evidence of an Italian heritage. Anne Flynn was no stranger to the Bridewell herself, appearing in the dock inter- mittently on minor charges. I recall one day when she turned up at the Bridewell and asked a garda, 'Am I up today?' I replied from the bench, 'No, you were up three days ago, and I issued a warrant for you.' She looked put out and said, 'Fuck it, I could have been uptown shoplifting', which amused me. Her husband would go on to serve the longest sentence imposed in the history of the state for drug dealing.

There was a clear pattern emerging before me at this time, and it related to drugs, mainly heroin. My middle-class upbringing had insulated me from street dealing, but now I was on a steep learning curve that added many new words to my vocabulary, I can tell you. The city was awash with illegal drugs, and the gardaí were working day and night to follow the trails back to the key suppliers and dealers. I saw it again and again from the bench of the Bridewell: with people like Felloni, it was the greed and the utter ruthlessness; with the young criminals, it was the addiction, the desperation, the horrible family circumstances and the promise the drugs seemed to hold at first – followed by the crashing reality of crime, arrest and prison. It was a far cry from my own upbringing on Dublin's

Southside, and I knew it was going to take time and care for me to learn what was happening in these lives, and why.

I had a famous accused in the dock in the Bridewell during this time: the singer Phil Lynott. He was brought up on a drugs charge, but his solicitor put forward a very persuasive argument as to Lynott's contrition and the necessity for his record to remain unblemished so that he could tour in America. He was a young man, with what could be a wonderful creative life before him, so I struck out the charge and let him off with a donation to charity via the court poor box. Within a year of that hearing, Lynott died of an overdose. When I heard the news, I did briefly question my judgment. What if a prison sentence had turned him around and saved his life? He was only 36 when he died – such a terrible waste. But I quickly realised that my job was to make the best decision with the available information, and that any thoughts of 'what if?' would derail me and prevent me from doing that job. I had to work with what was in front of me, make a conscientious, thoughtful decision and then stand over it – even when tragedy struck, as it did for this talented young man. The what-ifs were entirely unhelpful, that's what I quickly realised from that case.

The lack of training for judges did have consequences on the bench – as evidenced by my mishandling of the John Gilligan stealing/receiving case. The law is a vast and sprawling network of acts, clauses and subclauses, and it takes time to get a handle on it. I certainly made mistakes in those early weeks and months at the Bridewell. But it wasn't always a case of the judge making an outright mistake – sometimes we were led by the nose by those who should have behaved better.

The worst example of this in my own early career occurred when I was only weeks on the criminal bench at the Bridewell and still scrambling to learn the ropes. I can still picture the court that day: four young gardaí on my right-hand side and a woman in her fifties in the dock, up on charges relating to road traffic offences. Her solicitor was in front of my bench, and I knew him by reputation because he was very experienced and highly regarded. The case was called by the registrar, and the solicitor immediately got to his feet and commenced a long and detailed account of why this case was not being properly pursued by An Garda. He stated that a summons was required in such road traffic offences, that the matter was not for this court, where most criminal matters were dealt with differently, and that this incorrect procedure had to be halted right now. I had two problems: I was ignorant on the points of law he had raised, and I allowed myself to be swayed into thinking that he must be right because his was such a respected legal mind. That was two strikes against me. The third strike was that I didn't think to hear evidence from the assembled gardaí, who looked on tight-lipped and tense as the solicitor argued at great length. And thus I committed my terrible mistake: I struck out the case. That was that, and the solicitor and his client went out happily.

I was later told that the woman was the notorious Ma Nolan, the biggest receiver of stolen goods in the city and very well known to the gardaí. She had been evading summonses for some time, prompting the gardaí to try a different tack: charge her with the various offences and bring her to my court. In fact, I only found out there was a warrant in recent months – I was completely unaware of it on the day or afterwards. Well, that was a major lesson for a new judge: do not always trust a solicitor representing a criminal. I allowed him to draw a picture in my mind, and I trusted the picture rather than my own gut instinct. Looking back, it galls me now because he made a fool of me. I was new and I was a woman, and he played his hand for all he was worth, and I fell for it. I think that must count as my worst performance on the bench in my career. I can see it so clearly in my mind even today, and I want to shout at myself to wake up and pay attention, but of course it's too late for that. As I said, the what-ifs simply don't count.

About two years after the Ma Nolan hearing, a case came before me in Kilmainham, where I was then sitting. I was known for my sharp photographic memory in those days, although age has robbed me of that now. In came the garda in charge of the case, Garda John Hynes, and I recognised him instantly as one of the four gardaí who had stood silently by, helpless, as I was bamboozled by Ma Nolan's solicitor. I felt that sting of regret again and resolved to do something about it. I had him brought over to me, and I said to him, 'I have to apologise. I was wrong, you were right, and I did you and your colleagues a disservice.' I was well aware by then that an experience like that could make a young garda not want to return to court, which would be a very bad outcome. I was also aware that I could have adversely affected their careers. I had no problem admitting that and saying sorry, but I could tell that he was absolutely shocked to be receiving an apology from a judge. John and I are friends to this day, and he sometimes still shakes his head and chuckles about 'the only judge who ever apologised'. I might not be proud that I had to apologise, but I am very proud to be known as a judge who isn't afraid to own up and say sorry. I've no problem apologising, and I find it gets easier as you get older.

This touches on something about the role of judge that has long bothered me. I cannot abide the idea that judges are somehow 'up there', above everyone else in their chair positioned at a height. That is nonsense. Judges are not above the law any more than anyone else. I saw myself as facilitating justice, nothing more. I wasn't a special person because I had 'District Court Judge' before my name, I was just another court worker striving to deliver justice as best I could. The wigs, the gowns, the bowing and scraping... it's all claptrap. Judges are human, some are better at their jobs than others, and all of them make mistakes. I, for one, think we should apologise when we get it wrong. I think that if judges feel a sense of entitlement or elevation, it gets in the way of their learning – which is the core element of doing their job well. This was something I saw again and again among my colleagues, and I did not want to fall into that same trap of thinking I was somehow imbued with wisdom and therefore didn't need to listen and learn. I took a different attitude, and I can actually remember the moment when that mindset crystallised for me.

In my first weeks in the Bridewell, I was looking at a young man standing accused in the dock, and a thought cropped up in my mind: *If this young man was my son, or my grandson, what would I want the judge to know about him, ask him about, consider and care about?* I needed to know the answer to that. In order to find it, I did something unprecedented at that time. I contacted a probation

LESSONS FROM THE BENCH

officer and asked her to arrange a prison visit for me. I wanted to find out how prisoners fared, why they ended up in prison and if there was anything that could be done to help them. I have zero regrets about imprisoning criminals, let me be quite clear on that, but I wanted to be sure that it was the best solution in any given case. So out I went to Mountjoy Prison, or The Joy, in Phibsborough. There, I met Governor John Lonergan and began what turned out to be a wonderful friendship. John taught me so much. He invited me to view workshops and attend annual plays and concerts in The Joy. I went along to everything and chatted to so many men about their lives and what had brought them to this juncture. There was always joking and slagging when I visited Mountjoy. As you can imagine, I was a queasily familiar face to many of the people residing there. I remember one fellow came up and asked me for my autograph. I can assure you that is the only time in my life I have been approached for an autograph. I shook my head and said no – then asked him if he was in for forgery.

Those fascinating and insightful visits formed a hugely important part of increasing my empathy and understanding, which were crucial elements to my work. They also showed me that community services and projects could be extremely effective and an alternative to prison, and I brought that insight with me into the courtroom. I'm very glad I took that step, because it meant I did view every person in the dock as just that – a person, a fellow human being – and I treated them accordingly. In this way, the bench taught me as much about life as it did about the law. I came to realise that I had known little about either prior to being appointed a judge. All those times I had scuttled down the quays on my way to the Four Courts as a solicitor, I was rubbing shoulders with criminals as I went. They weren't set-apart people and they didn't wear signs that declared them to be 'bad' – they were just ordinary people, and the only difference between us was that I'd had different opportunities and made different choices in life.

Again, I can recall the moment when I realised this emphatically. I was walking to the Bridewell, and outside I met a young couple who had both appeared in my dock. The young woman suffered with Crohn's disease and was unwell; he was supporting her. I smiled and stopped to find out how they were doing. I remember feeling slightly surprised at myself in that moment, realising that I was chatting to them like friends, as if we weren't judge and accused. But it was the right thing to do. To my mind, it's part of effective policing and justice that we know each other and treat each other respectfully. None of this holier-than-thou judge guff.

This was very much reinforced for me by an important encounter in the Bridewell. It was a Friday afternoon after a long week, and a young man was in custody, charged with assaulting a security guard at a shopping centre. The court was full and noisy. Out of the press of bodies, a one-legged man on crutches slowly made his way to the witness box. He turned to me and said, 'Can I look into your lovely blue eyes?' I looked at him and said, 'If you insist.' That man was John Hardy, a youth worker based in Coolock, and I would come to know him and his family very well. That day, he spoke to me about the young man in the dock, about his life, his nature and the incident that had led to him standing before me. I looked over at the young man and was struck by how he hid behind his fringe. It grew down over his eyes, and he shot pained glances at me from under it. Then a woman came into the witness box and was introduced as the accused's mother. She asked me, 'Can I speak to you woman to woman?' That put my hackles up. I hated any reference to my gender as a basis for discussion or argument. However, I let her say her piece. In the end, I asked the young man to come back on Monday. I then had a miserable weekend, worrying about what to do. Prison? A second chance? Who should I trust? I lost sleep over it, which was a rare occurrence for me. I didn't know who to ask for advice or how to reach a decision.

The accused came back to court on Monday, and I took a slightly cowardly way out by putting back the case, releasing him and requesting a probation report. John Hardy was present again, and he assured me that he would look after the young man in the meantime. He invited me to visit Coolock and see for myself the work they were doing there. I agreed. That was the first time I ever went to visit someone I had met in the dock. I drove out to Coolock Garda Station, and a garda drove me to the young man's workplace at Coláiste Dhúlaigh, where he was doing community service. Thanks to John Hardy's encouragement, I visited regularly over the next 12 months, observing what a second chance looked like close up. On every visit, the young man peered at me from under that curtain of hair, unable to look me in the eye. On one visit, after I had been deposited at Coláiste Dhúlaigh, the garda car was hit by a rock. It hit the window exactly where I had been sitting and smashed it. The garda driver was extremely alert and had the young fella who threw the missile in court two days later.

I kept going out there, though. There were people like John Hardy all across the communities, quietly helping, persisting even when the odds were against them. I admired them – and John – immensely. Later, I took to calling John 'the Pied Piper', because all the children would run along behind him, eager to be around him and his reliable kindness. He was a force for good, that man, and he never looked for any recognition or reward for it.

When, one year later, the young man finally stood up straight, raised his head, pushed back his fringe and looked me in the eye as we spoke, I knew that was down to John's hard work and perseverance. He was so valuable to the people of Coolock, and he helped so many who would otherwise have been dismissed or forgotten. He worked tirelessly, and as a result young men, like that young man, came out of a life of crime, and their lives were changed for good. The moment when that young man raised his head and looked at me, that really did something to me. It said to me: *Keep going. It works.* He was the first young man I engaged with in this way, and it set the scene for all the rest. I'm very grateful to John Hardy for that early lesson. That experience laid the all-important foundation stone upon which so many of my judgments on the criminal bench were based over the next two decades.

CHAPTER 3

SOMETIMES A PUNISHMENT
CAN BRING ITS OWN REWARDS

The Bridewell was a hugely stimulating and challenging place to work because I was learning all the time. This was an entirely new world for a woman of my background and age, and I had to work hard to keep up with all the new information sweeping through the court every day. It helped that I was naturally interested in people, but I also had to decide to engage in this manner and commit to it. I quickly learned that poverty and upbringing were key factors in the lives of so many criminals, but that drugs had a much wider catchment area and took in people of all hues and stripes. I knew by now that I really enjoyed the criminal bench of the District Court, primarily because all of human life came through its doors in a way I found unpredictable and exhilarating. But my president, Tommy Donnelly, wanted me to gain experience of other courts as well, which is why, in December 1984, I was moved out of the Bridewell and into Smithfield Children Court.

Smithfield was a modern building with only one courtroom and, unlike ordinary courts, the public were not allowed in to witness the proceedings. If a defendant entered a not guilty plea, then there had to be a hearing with the victim present. The court heard cases concerning defendants aged up to 18 years, but their crimes weren't shocking to me. In fact, I have very little recollection of the hearings there. I think that's because I was focused on what I needed to learn and also because I had no knowledge of the youngsters before me or their backgrounds. Those insights would come later, but for now it was a procession of similar-looking youngsters who had lost their path, one way or another. I was at sea myself, trying to get to grips with the nuances of the juvenile court. And in the end, it turned out to be a short-lived posting.

In February 1985, Tommy Donnelly announced that he would retire as president of the District Court at the end of the month. He would be sadly missed. Looking back now, there were some presidents I wouldn't let run my household, let alone the District Court service, but Tommy was one of the very best in that role in my time. After the announcement, Tommy called me in to see him. He told me that he was moving me out of Smithfield because if he didn't do it before he left, I would be stuck there for my whole career. I have no doubt he was right. The Children Court would have been seen as an ideal post for a woman judge, and no one would have questioned it. So, my president made another prescient decision and moved me out to Dún Laoghaire District Court, which was also part of the Dublin Metropolitan District but covered all case types – civil, criminal and licensing. Neither he nor I could ever have guessed what would happen next, nor how it would eventually affect my career.

I believe I was sent to Dún Laoghaire primarily to solve a problem that was generating many complaints at that time. The sitting judge was very slow in his work – though no doubt he would have said methodical. His courts sometimes ran on until 10 p.m., and the other court staff were getting fed up with the long hours. So, seeing that I had experience under my belt from the Bridewell, Tommy sent me out there. It was very different from Smithfield and the juvenile court, but I very much enjoyed working there.

At the time, Dún Laoghaire District Court was based in the old courthouse, which was next to the garda station. It was a fine old building, with steps up to an impressive front door, although we used the side door to go in and out to work. The yard behind the courthouse was shared with the garda station, so it was always a hive of activity. It was a busy District Court, hearing cases of all kinds, from summonses for road traffic offences to murder. It was smaller than the Bridewell, but it had that same bustling atmosphere of people constantly on the move. I was still in my learning phase about the criminal fraternity back then, and I blush now to think of my naivety. I remember being struck by the number of defendants appearing before me who hailed from various parts of Dublin and north of the city, some of which I would have dealt with in the Bridewell. I wondered how they managed the logistics of committing crimes out in Dún Laoghaire. It was gently pointed out to me that everyone in the dock came from places accessible along the DART train line. I'm sure my colleagues must have smiled at having to explain that obvious connection to me. I may as well have been wearing L-plates.

What I had been observing in the Bridewell was reinforced in the courtroom at Dún Laoghaire: certain areas of Dublin suffered from a level of social deprivation that created all manner of problems, some of which ended up in the courthouse. There were neighbourhoods that were grossly over-represented in the courtroom. It wasn't that all of the crime-inclined people had opted to live near each other – it was an indication of inadequate social policy. That was becoming clearer and clearer to me as time went on.

I had one case there that really stayed with me because it was very different from the normal run of cases – and involved a different postcode, for a change – and it made me wonder how well you could ever know another person. The case was scheduled to start on 27 March 1985 and my first inkling of this not being a run-of-the-mill case came when a senior garda arrived in from next door one morning. He told me that the prisoner being brought in that afternoon would arrive to a packed and bewildered court. He was forewarning me. Naturally, I was very curious about who was going to come through the doors that afternoon.

As predicted, the court was packed tight for the afternoon session. I had never seen the place swarming with so many bodies and it was rather daunting for a relatively new judge, as I then was. I watched as the gardaí escorted into the room a man I remember as having a beard and a very mature demeanour: well dressed, well groomed and like a fish out of water in his present surroundings. At his entrance, the courtroom fell silent, and every head turned to watch him make his way to the front. I could see the wide-eyed stares and could sense that people were shocked and upset. The man, an American by birth, was described as a much-respected member of the Dalkey community, and

I think three-quarters of the town's population was in the court that day. He was married to an Irish woman and had a wide network of friends, all of whom had been stunned by the news that he had been arrested on a charge of murder. The atmosphere was electrically charged, and all I could do was pay close attention and aim for a solid and sensible judgment on whatever matter was going to unfold before me.

The man, who gave his name as Michael O'Shea, was accused of murdering his first wife in Rochester, New York, in 1967, by poisoning her with wood alcohol that he put into a cocktail he served to her. It was alleged he did this during their child's fifth birthday party. The case set out that he had been arrested for the crime in America and imprisoned, but had escaped from a hospital while undergoing psychiatric testing. He had then made his way to Ireland in and around the early 1970s, where he had begun the second chapter of his life with a clean slate.

After a burglary at his Dalkey home, Michael O'Shea had called the gardaí to investigate. The detectives had to ascertain which fingerprints belonged to the family and which to the burglar, so they took fingerprints from everyone, with a view to a process of elimination. To their astonishment, O'Shea's fingerprints turned up a match to a man who had been sentenced to life for murder in America. That man was called Joseph Michael Maloney. When this was put to Michael O'Shea, he was adamant that he knew nothing of any of this and that he was, and only ever had been, Michael O'Shea.

Here, I must confess that my recollection of that day is patchy, so I had to check articles written at the time for the details. While I don't recall it, apparently a retired detective from New York gave evidence in my court. Detective George Reis was also a former neighbour of the accused, and he testified that the man in the dock was, in fact, Joseph Michael Maloney, not Michael O'Shea as he claimed – and that he was indeed the very man who had been tried and convicted of murder.

The press of bodies in the courtroom listened in rapt silence as all of this was relayed – and I did, too, because it was fascinating to hear this alternative life story of the well-groomed and obviously well-liked man before me. I kept wondering about his present wife and how she had handled being told this disturbing history about the man she thought she knew. It must be a surreal experience to have someone you love suddenly become an entirely unknown person before your eyes as their past unravels.

Based on the evidence, I ordered his extradition to the USA. The Irish-American extradition treaty had only been in effect for about 14 weeks at that point, and this man was just the fourth person extradited under its terms. That was my first and last contact with Joseph Michael Maloney, because he never turned up in my court again. But that wasn't the end of his story.

Before Maloney's extradition could be carried out, a technical legal issue arose with the Irish-American treaty. The upshot of this glitch was that in July 1986, the Supreme Court directed that Maloney be released. He left Mountjoy Jail a free man – but he didn't return to the bosom of Dalkey. No one knows where he went. The extradition treaty was ironed out in early 1987 and his warrant was reactivated, but to no avail. There was no trace of him to be found. Wherever he went, whoever might have helped him, Maloney had made good his escape. To this day, he remains at large, still a wanted man – under my extradition warrant. A strange end to a strange case.

I would happily have stayed in Dún Laoghaire, but there were moves afoot behind the scenes that would end that particular posting. Unbeknown to me, the judge whose place I had taken paid a visit to the newly appointed president of the District Court, Oliver Macklin – known to all as Puffer because of a respiratory condition. The judge asked to be reinstated in Dún Laoghaire and, without making any enquiries, Puffer readily agreed. I was called in and simply told that I was going back to the Bridewell, no explanation given. I didn't request one. I said goodbye to Dún Laoghaire and headed back into Court 4 at the Bridewell once again.

I continued to work and learn and was doing very well there. I knew President Macklin was pleased with me because that Christmas he asked me to stay in the Bridewell until July 1986, to which I replied, 'Yes, please.' He sent me a letter to confirm this agreement. But it wasn't long after Christmas that we hit a major problem. There was a solicitor in the Bridewell who was making very good money because his services were in great demand. I had heard that another colleague of mine was jealous of this situation. He had set out his grievances to Puffer, who decreed that I should operate a rota system for solicitors, whereby as each case came up, it would be handed to the next solicitor on the list. I queried the legality of this, since it is the right of the defendant to request a specific, preferred solicitor. I said to Puffer, 'I don't think you can do that.'

The reason I said that was due to a legal precedent set in an old case whose title I can easily remember because it always made me smile: Sherry vs Wine. That case had examined this very issue of the right to choose a solicitor, and the relevant regulations specifically indicated that it should be a solicitor of the defendant's choice. That was the precedent I was leaning on when I went against Puffer and told him that we could not operate a rota system. I was correct, but that didn't matter.

There was a postscript added to the letter I had received from President Macklin just before Christmas, which read: *Use rota system*. I had seen

the note, but then I genuinely forgot about it. I
suppose the defendant's right to choose a solicitor
was so ingrained in my thinking, this new edict
didn't stick in my brain. In all cases from January to
Easter, I repeatedly granted the solicitor requested
by the defendant without realising my 'error'. No
one ever spoke to me about it, but it was noticed.

Each year, I would take my holidays at Easter,
adding on three days to the normal court closure
to spend time with my family. In 1986, I was on
my annual break as usual when I received a phone
call from work on the Thursday after Easter. The
registrar was calling to tell me that she'd heard I
wasn't coming back to the Bridewell and to wish
me well. That was news to me. As far as I was
concerned, I was sitting in Court 4 on Monday.

The next day I received a letter telling me to
attend at the Central Mission Court on Lower
Abbey Street the following week. That court heard
cases to do with parking fines and the like, so it was
a step down from the Bridewell in my eyes. After
one week there, I was told to report to Court 1 at
Morgan Place, where summonses were dealt with.
After one week there, I was told to report to Court

3 at Morgan Place, where my job was to hear more summonses. After three weeks of being shunted from court to court, I decided to go and speak to my president and find out what was happening. I hadn't a clue why I was suddenly pitching up at a different court every week and hearing summonses and fines.

I went to Puffer's office and asked him why I was being moved around, given that we had an agreement that I would sit in the Bridewell until July. I asked if I had done something wrong, if he was displeased with my work for some reason, or if he felt I wasn't up to the criminal bench. He replied, 'I don't have to tell you.' That was an unexpected retort, and I was quite taken aback. I tried again. I told him that I needed him to tell me so that I could learn from my mistake, whatever it was. He replied, 'It's a matter of conscience.' Suddenly, the penny dropped with clanging clarity. I looked at him in disbelief and said, 'You don't mean the solicitor rota thing, do you?' He did not reply, but his expression said it all. I was disgusted. I clicked my heels and walked out of the room. That was an absolutely huge thing for me to do because it was very much beyond the bounds of expected civil behaviour. I had never clicked my heels and walked out on someone before – and I've never done it since. It sounds a minor reaction, but it was in fact a measure of just how angry I was. He would have been deeply shocked by this display, I've no doubt. I was a bit shocked at myself, to be honest. But I was past caring because, to my mind, his behaviour was entirely unacceptable.

I was incensed by the whole incident. There was no valid reason for his anger towards me: the solicitor rota did not follow the law, and I had proved myself again and again at Dún Laoghaire and at the Bridewell as a competent and professional judge of the District Court. I could not respect his inability to talk to me directly about the issue, and I resented the fact that he had waited until my annual Easter recess to drop the guillotine. I saw that as both disrespectful and cowardly.

Not long after that meeting, I received my next week-long posting: Kilmainham District Court. A lot of things were going through my mind when I was told that I was headed for the criminal bench at Kilmainham. I was now very aware that this was a reprimand from Puffer for what he felt was unacceptable behaviour, a punishment for not toeing the line. I knew that Kilmainham was seen as a challenging post – indeed I had recollections of it from my own early years as a young solicitor in the late 1950s – and I knew it was an immensely busy court that some found a bit overwhelming. Was I nervous? No, I don't think so. I don't think I felt anything positive or negative about Kilmainham. I saw it as a job that I had to go and do. I was more seasoned by now, of course, because I was used to the criminal bench, so that helped too. Plus, the letter told me that I would be there for only one week, just like my other punishment postings, so I wouldn't be settling in there.

Meanwhile, back at Court 4 in the Bridewell, my sudden disappearance had been the subject of much discussion. Imagine my surprise when some of the solicitors there approached me to offer thanks for my stance on the rota system. They invited me out to dinner and explained that they were in full agreement with me that it was illegal, and they explained their plan of action. They were going to wait until an appropriate case presented itself and then state a case to the High Court that would require that court to pronounce on the legality or otherwise of the rota system. They were confident they would win. They appreciated the fact that I hadn't given in to Puffer and had queried the system he was determined to put in place.

It took about two and a half years for the Bridewell solicitors' case to come up at the High Court, but eventually it did. And they did win. The High Court confirmed that it was the defendant's legal right to choose their own solicitor and that therefore a rota system could not be put in place. Puffer had left me at Kilmainham throughout those two and a half years. Even before I was posted there, a judge on the bench at Kilmainham had developed a drinking problem, and I was the easy, on-hand solution. (It was a coincidence that the judge in question was the same one who had christened me 'that bitch Hussey'.) In 1988, Puffer retired. His successor was Peter Smithwick, whom I knew from college. By then, I was very at home in Kilmainham and had become involved in various community projects. I paid a visit to Smithwick at his office in the Four Courts and asked his permission to stay on at Kilmainham for six more months, since I wanted to follow through on the We Have A Dream (WHAD) youth project in Ballyfermot, in particular. He agreed to my request.

Kilmainham deserved its reputation as a challenging court. My first impression was that it was like a mart – always noisy, constantly busy, with sudden shouts of swearing and bursts of laughter equally common. It covered a huge area, stretching from Camden Street in Dublin 2 to Leixlip in County Kildare, and taking in Ballyfermot, Clondalkin, Lucan, Leixlip, Rathcoole and Ronanstown, the funnel point for three separate garda districts. As a result, it was inundated with cases, and we worked extremely hard to keep the huge legal juggernaut rolling day to day. It also meant that court reporters were a daily feature, because there was always something happening, some juicy nugget to report back to the outside world. Presiding over a court of this size and busyness required razor-sharp mental focus and a high level of stamina. I quickly realised that I absolutely loved it.

I had learned from the Bridewell that the cells could be underneath the court, and it was no different in Kilmainham. There were male and female cells down below, with a set of granite stone steps leading up into the courtroom. I was told it was best to tackle those steps drunk! Kilmainham is unique in that it is located right beside the old gaol, with a tunnel running directly between the two, although it was disused in my day. Beside the courtroom, I had a beautiful chamber – spacious and well appointed. It was my sanctuary from the madness outside, and I cherished it.

By now, I felt I had a good insight into the workings of the District Court and the people who came through it. I was starting to develop my own ideas of justice and how best to serve it. In particular, I had decided that the best approach to any judgment was to look beyond the criminal act to the person and their circumstances. I wasn't interested in the big-name criminals. They often can't be changed or saved. I was interested in the meat of the District Court, namely those ordinary cases and criminals that filed through day after day. It was among that cohort that it might be possible to intervene and put someone on a different path. That was why I had a particular affinity for young criminals and always sought to find out if they would respond to an alternative to prison. The aim was to be fair, but tough. If they needed a spell in prison, I was happy to hand out a sentence. But if there was a chink in their armour that suggested the light could get through, I was also happy to use all of the tools at my disposal, such as the Probation Service, to try to help them make different choices and leave the path they were on towards a life of crime.

The way I looked at it was that if we could pull someone back off that path, we were all winners – the accused, the gardaí who had to spend time on them, the families involved and the taxpayer, who was saved the cost of an additional resident in the prison system. Sometimes jail was the best way to get through to a repeat offender, but it wasn't ever going to be a satisfactory long-term solution for society, not with these types of relatively low-level criminals. What I loved about the work in Kilmainham was that I saw the same people, got to know them and sometimes point them in the direction of help, and I could gauge how they were getting on and what might work for them. Best of all, when a young person did decide to change, to

choose a different way, I often got to see that, too –
the end of the story, or a new beginning, depending
on your point of view. To me, the criminals who
came through Kilmainham every day of the week
were my family. I know that sounds odd, but it was
how I saw it: we were a big court family – messy,
noisy, sometimes succeeding, sometimes failing.
God love them, their own families were often a
huge part of their problem, so I was glad to present
an alternative.

I may have been sent to Kilmainham as a
punishment, but I had unexpectedly found my home
and my purpose. I was a District Court judge to my
bones – I knew that now. I remember when the rule
was changed in the 1990s, meaning that solicitors,
as well as barristers, were allowed to become higher
courts judges. Many people said to me, 'You'll go
for that, won't you?' My reply was always the
same: 'Over my dead body.' There was no way I
would leave those young offenders, those ordinary
criminals, those who could be helped to change
by a court that understood its wider function. The
High Court is reverential, bewigged and begowned,
with a jury taking on the role of deciding guilt or

innocence. The performative side of it does not appeal to me at all. If I were a victim, I would be completely put off by how some of the barristers can behave in that setting. Give me the straight-forward practicality of the District Court any day. There, I was able to have more input and impact as a judge. I could track the effect and progress of my decisions by those who came through my court. It feels very up close and personal, with a sole judge listening and deciding, and that in itself fosters empathy. Once I had sampled life on the criminal bench, I knew that I rightly belonged in the noisy, teeming energy of the District Court.

Looking back on my 16-year career on the bench at Kilmainham now, I wonder if President Tommy Donnelly had the measure of me when he first put me on the criminal bench. I suppose, whether I sank or swam, we would both have learned something valuable about me as judge. The president's job is to match judges to courts, and I admire the fact that he was open to my match, regardless of my gender. I only wish I'd known then what I know now, so I could have asked him about it. For years, I marvelled at his crazy decision, but now I wonder if he saw what I couldn't see: that I had it in me to be a decent judge on the criminal bench.

It was very different with President Oliver Macklin, of course. He placed me in Kilmainham to teach me a different kind of lesson – about obeying authority. If only he'd known that he was dealing with the only girl in the history of Loreto College Foxrock to fail her religion exam! I was suspicious of the hail-fellow-well-met act of the priest who instructed us, who used to do things like throw chalk playfully at girls to indicate he was choosing them to answer a question. I would sit back in my chair with narrowed eyes and judge him harshly for his frivolous behaviour. The priest was a good-looking man, and the rest of my classmates responded well to him. I didn't. His attitude put me off completely and I didn't engage with his teaching at all. As a result, I failed the exam – an unheard-of occurrence for me and for the subject. I carry that exam failure as a mark of pride. And, to be honest, I carry my reprimand from Puffer as a mark of pride, too. Perhaps his action was that of an insecure person, but I felt the contempt contained within it, and I knew I didn't deserve that. Of course, it's funny to review all of this now, from the distance of old age, because being sent to Kilmainham was the very best thing that ever happened to me. I had 16 absolutely wonderful, happy years there, and I treasure them all. Thank you, Puffer!

CHAPTER 4

IF YOU WANT TO BE USEFUL, COMPASSION MUST BE BACKED BY UNDERSTANDING

Kilmainham in the 1980s and '90s was the Spaghetti Junction of the District Court system: a constant melee of people passed through its doors and corridors, and there wasn't a quiet corner to be found. It was about as far from the rarefied atmosphere of the higher courts as you could get. I relied heavily on my registrar to keep our courtroom moving efficiently, and over time I also got to know the many gardaí who spent time there. Slowly but surely, I built up a solid understanding of the people around me: who I could trust, who needed to be watched a bit more carefully, who would be straight with me and who might be prone to exaggeration. That was essential knowledge for me to be able to do my job well, and I was grateful to every member of the court who cooperated and helped the days to run as smoothly as possible.

Over time I learned that another type of understanding was also essential. As I developed my own concepts of what justice could and should entail, I realised that compassion was all well and good, but it was no use without understanding. Compassion is an important trait in a judge, but if the judge doesn't understand the lives and motivations of the people before them, then they are limited in their comprehension of the situation, of the crime and of the best course of action to recommend. It is understanding that moves you beyond simple empathy and that allows you to consider the accused, as well as the victim, in a meaningful way. I knew that I had to develop my understanding to a high level in order to be in a position to make good judgments.

The criminal compulsion was utterly alien to me as a 50-year-old middle-class woman. As far as

I was concerned, the people in the dock led lives I couldn't even picture. That's what made me realise that I would have to go out into their world, and I'd have to keep an open mind while I was there. I had been visiting Mountjoy Prison occasionally, thanks to John Lonergan's invitations, but that was the end point of the process. I started to wonder about all the points before that – the points where it might be possible to intervene and make a difference. For me, this meant going out into the community among the criminals, the victims, the gardaí and the probation officers and youth workers who tried to act as a bridge between these various elements. I had to go to see it all for myself, first-hand.

It quickly became obvious to me that the main causes of crime in my court were drugs and drug addiction. Illegal substances like heroin, cocaine and cannabis were all over Dublin at that time, and the area covered by the Kilmainham jurisdiction was particularly badly hit. Certain addresses, flats and street names in Dublin 8 and Dublin 10 came up again and again on the charge sheets, and I became well versed in them. The combination of poverty and lack of education, options and opportunities meant that many people sought solace in a high. And if they weren't looking for solace, they were looking for an income by dealing in the stuff. One way or another, it was often a direct path to the court door.

A priest in the inner city once said to me that he could 'put the number of their prison cell on their foreheads at baptism', such was the horrible inevitability of life for youngsters born in certain areas and to certain families. That statement struck me forcibly – the utter injustice and grimness of it. It was completely wrong in every way, and it galled me that it was regarded by many as simply 'the norm'. That's not the kind of birthright anyone wants to have – or wants their child to have.

I was chatting about this one day with Detective Tom Madden of the Drug Squad. This would have been in 1987, when I was relatively new to Kilmainham. I told him that I knew absolutely nothing about drugs, that his work was completely beyond me in terms of my own life experience and that this lack of insight was a problem in terms of doing my job well. In response, he invited me out on a night patrol with him and his colleague. I thought: *Why not?* As far as I was aware, this was a first for any judge, but someone had to lead the way. I'm sure some of my colleagues might have baulked at the suggestion, but it seemed like a good idea to me.

On the evening in question, I joined Tom and his colleague Pat Kirwan in their unmarked garda car. I sat in the back, feeling mysterious in an anorak with the hood up and a scarf covering my face. I was praying no one would spot me or recognise me, because I wasn't sure what the reaction to my escapade might be around the courts. Accordingly, I was travelling incognito – a watching brief.

Our first stop was Fitzwilliam Square, to talk to the women who plied their trade on the streets there. We parked, turned off the lights and observed. It was an eye-opener, I can tell you. The amount of cars with lone men in them driving round and round the square was quite shocking. The women were friendly with the gardaí and came over to the car to say hello to Tom and Pat. I was surprised that some spoke with English accents, but Tom explained that they came to Dublin from London and other English cities because they could make good money from a night's work here. Prostitution was very much a profession for them. There was no shortage of clients, that was for sure. Tom shook his head and remarked that those men we were watching would later go home to their wives.

I was fascinated that the women were so comfortable chatting to the gardaí, but then it was a mutually beneficial relationship: the gardaí gave them protection by keeping an eye on things, while the women could pass on nuggets of information gleaned through their work. It cut both ways, and each appreciated the other. I hadn't known that was how it worked, but it made sense once I saw it in action.

From Fitzwilliam Square we went across to Hawkins Street, where the rent boys worked. These were young men, often from broken families or tough backgrounds, who were struggling to keep life and limb together. Tom and Pat checked in on them and had a brief word with a few of them. Then we moved on to Palmerston Park, where gay male adult prostitutes waited in the shadows and their customers skulked along the railings. My final stop of the night was a house arrest on a drug-related charge. We brought that person to Terenure Garda Station, and when Tom and Pat went in to take care of the paperwork, I took my leave and headed off back to the world I knew best. For years afterwards, people would come up to me and tell me they'd heard a strange rumour about a judge and the Drug Squad patrol. Every time, I'd draw back my shoulders, eye them coldly and say, 'That's utter nonsense.' On the day of my retirement, in April 2002, in my farewell speech I admitted for the first time that it was all true.

I thought about all I'd seen that night for a long time. It was the same as my realisation that I had been walking among criminals all my life, rubbing shoulders with them on the streets – because they were just people like me. Here was a night-time Dublin that I had been blissfully unaware of, until now. While I lay in bed, poring over a good thriller or a Book of Evidence, safe and secure in my comfortable home, those men and women were out in the cold and the dark, trying to make a living and make it through the night in one piece. That trip into the night-time of the city was an absolute education for me, and an important one. It taught me about what was out there, about why people might seek solace in a substance, and about how easily you could fall between the cracks of self-medication and end up with an addiction. The stress of those lives, the fear and tension, the constant sense that things were just shy of unravelling out of control – living like that day in and day out would damage the hardiest of souls. It was a tough, tough life in a world that existed right beside my own but felt like it was aeons apart. It's strange how we exist side by side like that in society, so close and yet so far apart. Thinking all this, I felt I knew so much more after that one foray. It had proven to me that the courtroom doesn't teach you enough. It was essential to reach out beyond the walls and find out what was going on out there.

That's also why I was very open to visiting people's homes with the Probation Service. My long-time friend Liz O'Donoghue, a devoted probation officer, brought me out to Ballyfermot to meet families who knew all too much about the horrors of addiction. I visited the home of a woman who had an alcoholic husband and two sons who were drug addicts. The whole household was on the dole, drawing social welfare to survive. I was ignorant going into that house, but I emerged with a much clearer picture of the reasons why young men and women ended up in the dock in Kilmainham. There was a pattern that started in childhood and dogged them all the way to adulthood. But – and this was the really crucial part – people like Liz *were* making an impact and a difference. And that told me that I could help, too.

(I must add a small addendum to this story, which illustrates how Liz and her work truly did make a difference, even if it sometimes took years to come to fruition. In 2022, at the time of writing, Liz got in touch to say that one of those sons had asked to meet with me. He is now completely drug-free and running his own company and he wanted to talk to both of us. That, in itself, is a marvellous testament to Liz and the Probation Service. It gladdens my heart no end to hear it.)

I was seeing the raw end of drug use in my court all the time. There was a constant stream of addicts through the place, although I rarely saw anyone high in court. They were usually terribly young, only 19 or 20 years old; their uniform consisted of tracksuit and runners; and they shared a common story: damaging backgrounds causing a drift into petty crime, then into drugs. After that, it often went downhill – unless they could be caught and brought back on to a better path by the Probation Service and probably, for many, an addiction treatment centre. This was why I became passionate about the merits of the social services: because I could see the potential for saving these young adults from repeating this deadening pattern. From my vantage point in my judge's chair, I spotted one big agent of change in the lives of young male addicts: the good girlfriend. I'd often see the same young chap again and again, on minor but regular offences, and I'd be living in hope of a good girlfriend arriving on the scene. If they fell for a girl and she fell for them and made them feel good about themselves, it was amazing the difference it could make. It was as if they woke up, looked around and realised there was more to life than they'd ever considered before. I always rejoiced when I saw that happening.

Another facet of drug addiction that featured heavily in the courtroom concerned methadone. This is a heroin substitute, used to help wean addicts off the drug. The state set up day centres that dispense methadone to those who were prescribed it by a certified doctor. What I saw, though, was people who ended up hooked on methadone for years, swapping one addiction for another. To me, that's not the right approach. In addition, as with any of these things, it also brought in those who saw a chance to make money from it. I remember a girl who came before me, who was getting her methadone from a chemist in Dublin 8, when no other pharmacist would fill her script. The chemist in question was behaving in an unscrupulous manner, and people were arriving at his door from far and wide because it became known that he'd hand over methadone when other pharmacists and doctors wouldn't. He came up to give evidence in this case. I was aware of his game, and I disliked it. When he finished giving his evidence, he asked me, 'Can I go?' I looked across at him and said, 'You stay there. That's far better than what you're doing outside.' He was only there as a witness, but I took great pleasure in holding him there. It was a way of letting him know that I had no respect for him because of his callous behaviour.

I also recall visiting a new state-run residential treatment centre in Ballyfermot early one morning. I went up there with the local chief superintendent to see the premises before it opened for business. We were shown around by the head psychiatrist of the Health Board, as it was then. At one point he announced with ardent certainty, 'Of course, there will be no one here that will be appearing before the courts.' Neither of us replied, but later we had a good laugh at that notion. 'They will have no residents,' the chief superintendent said to me. We were both astonished at how little that psychiatrist knew about addiction and treatment. Clearly, I wasn't the only one with an awful lot to learn.

There was also the issue of alcohol addiction, of course, but in Ireland that had been classed as harmless for a long time. People spoke about alcohol in a completely different way from illegal substances and prescription drugs. There was a sort of exasperated but affectionate tone when they spoke about someone 'liking the drink', which could be a euphemism for everything – from being embarrassingly tipsy, to being violent and incoherent. I couldn't ever understand it, because alcohol addiction ripped families apart up and down the country. It is a miserable and terribly damaging existence to be the child of an alcoholic, a haunting legacy that often lasts a lifetime. I was lucky in that regard because my mother's family were nearly all alcoholics, but she escaped the same fate – which means I did, too. I'm convinced that the only reason she didn't succumb to alcoholism was my father's iron will on the subject. He was very strict about socialising and drinking. The only time he loosened the reins was at Christmas, and I can remember my mother being tipsy at my uncle's annual festive get-together. But that was the only time in the year I ever saw her like that. The other 364 days, my father made sure there was no alcohol in the house and certainly no tippling. At least, he thought he made sure, but I often found a half-full bottle of sherry in a cupboard in the kitchen!

The drug addicts never came to court high, but the alcoholics would often be at some level of inebriation, ranging from smiling to roaring. There was a well-known chronic alcoholic who was on first-name terms with the gardaí and all of us in the court. On one occasion he was charged, yet again, with being drunk and disorderly, but he didn't show up, which was unusual for him. I issued a bench warrant for his arrest. I later discovered that the day before he was due in my court, he had appeared at the Central Criminal Court as a witness. It was a murder case – the body of a woman had been found in the boot of a car, if memory serves, which it often doesn't at my age. This man was long-term homeless, so he used to spend day and night on the streets. As it happened, he was lying on the street nearby when the murderer was dumping the body, and he saw everything, while passing unseen himself. That made him the key witness for the prosecution. By all accounts, he turned up and did his job in the dock well: the defendant was found guilty, and the gardaí were thrilled with the outcome. I put two and two together and reckoned that he possibly hadn't turned up in my court because he had been royally entertained by the gardaí the night before!

There were many cases of drunk and disorderly on the daily roll call at Kilmainham – usually older men, lifelong drunks, and it was impossible to get through to them. My approach was to put them in custody for a week, because it meant they'd get three square meals a day and sleep in a proper bed, under a roof. I felt it was the charitable thing to do, and I never minded the taxpayer footing the bill for it. All I could do for these chronic addicts was to give them a little respite from their grim lives. They looked pathetic, and I felt a week's 'holiday' in custody was a small help to them. When I retired, a lovely lady called Alice Leahy arrived to court at 9.30 a.m. on my last day. I was surprised and very touched when she handed me a posy of African violets and thanked me on behalf of all the homeless men I'd put in custody. Alice runs a homeless centre behind Dublin Castle, and she was aware that I had these men's best interests at heart. It was a wonderful moment, not least because it can be so hard to know if what you're doing is the right thing, or if it is making any difference at all. You question yourself constantly as a judge. But with that kind gesture, Alice let me know that my treatment of those men was right and appreciated.

At the start of my career, there wasn't much in the way of dedicated help for addicts, but that changed over the course of my 16 years at Kilmainham. I was an early admirer and supporter of Coolmine

Addiction Centre, and I would recommend a probation report in any case where I felt there was a chance of an accused being ready to change their ways. I couldn't order anyone to attend an addiction centre – that wasn't within my powers – but I knew that the probation officers would soon discern if there was an appetite for change and they would recommend that course of action, which was my motive in sending people their way. If there was no appetite for change, it was jail, no apologies.

I greatly admired the work Coolmine was doing. I even developed my own 'Coolmine Days': four or five times a year, I would spend the day out there talking to the residents, finding out what was happening for them and how the treatments worked. The average residential stay was between 12 and 18 months, so it took great dedication and determination to stay the course and become a 'former addict'. It was so encouraging to see how many people achieved that. I often said to the people I met there that no one took greater delight in their transformation than I did. They knew – and I knew – how easy it was to fall off the wagon and lapse into old habits, and how hard it was to get up every day and choose not to do that. I was deeply impressed by those who had the staying power and the will to go the distance.

Over time, I noticed that the men accused of the more serious crimes – such as robbery and assault, which I would send forward to the higher courts – would often go to Coolmine of their own accord while on bail and waiting for the Book of Evidence to be compiled, a process that could take a long time. They had known it was there – and indeed the Probation Service might have sent them out there before – but as is the way with addiction, one day the switch would flick, and they'd finally be ready to quit. It only dawned on me years later that this set in place a precedent whereby many defendants got help at Coolmine before their case reached the higher courts. As a result, they arrived in court with a guilty plea and proof that their addiction was under control. This, in turn, meant that they ended up with a lesser or suspended sentence. I see now that this saved the state a lot of money and did everyone a service – even if I wasn't aware of that at the time. One positive action led to another, and it eased the burden all round.

I always enjoyed the Christmas Day festivities in Coolmine. One year, during my Christmas visit, a chap who was only too well known to me came over and shyly handed me a card. Inside, he had written the loveliest sentiments. I joked with him that it must have been the first card he hadn't nicked. And I was particularly struck by a man who came up to me one Christmas Day and thanked me sincerely, saying that, were it not for me, he'd still be on the streets, or dead. Again, that reinforced my approach and told me to keep believing in people's ability to change.

I think I related to addicts and was able to engage with them because I recognised something of myself in them. I came from a time in Ireland when we didn't have knowledge of or ready access to illegal substances, apart from *poitín*. That only changed around the end of the 1960s, when the underground economy in narcotics started to take off. However, we did have legal, over-the-counter drugs. For as long as I can remember, I would hear older people talking about their nightly sleeping pills, much depended upon and guaranteed by a long-term prescription from their GP. I was reminded of that when I noted how many drug addicts in my court were hung up on sleeping pills. I remember one chap had four prescriptions with four different chemists, so essential were the pills to him.

I also recall having Valium pushed on me by my own GP when I was a young housewife, even when I said no, thank you. 'Mother's little helper' was a popular and acceptable drug, and GPs were quick to put it into women's hands back then. It was easy to see how psychological dependence could take hold. The addicts I was meeting had the same problem, just with a different substance. The good people of Ireland would have been shocked at the idea of being classed as addicts, but they were in fact addicted to those little boosts to their systems. The difference is that they didn't have to commit crimes to get their fix, and society viewed their need for these substances as perfectly acceptable. The longer I spent in Kilmainham, the more I realised that this is really just a smokescreen, because it all comes from the same human impulse.

According to society, as a judge I was 'above' the people in the dock, I was 'different', I was 'better'. I was in my eye! I used to laugh at myself, because I'd spend the morning hearing drug cases and all kinds of crime associated with them, and the moment court went into recess at 1 p.m., I'd rush straight to my chamber for a much-needed cigarette. I knew that was an addiction, too, which put me on a par with the people whose names appeared on the charge sheets. The reason I understood and was deeply interested in addiction and its treatment was partly down to having an addictive personality myself.

I had come late to smoking, taking it up in 1959 when I was 22 years old, and I loved it. I was working in my first job, with a room to myself, and one day, out of the blue, I thought to myself: *Shall I buy a pack of cigarettes?* So I did. From then on, I smoked 20 a day – never more than that – and was never without a 20 pack in my pocket. I began to develop chest problems, but I soldiered on – because I was hooked. In 1996 I went for a golf weekend with some gardaí friends over in Oughterard, County Galway, and I smoked myself silly. After work, on Monday, I went to my GP, having managed to snag the last appointment of the day. We knew each other well, and it was a relaxed and chatty appointment given that the waiting room was now empty. He diagnosed bronchitis and proceeded to lecture me about smoking. He said I'd have to give up. I retorted, 'Have you?' His reply irritated me deeply: 'I have it under control. I smoke three a day.' Well, that answer provoked my stubborn streak, which has always been a mile wide. I thought to myself: *Damn you, I can control it too.* I absolutely hated the idea of being seen as weak-willed.

On my way to Kilmainham the following morning, I stopped at the usual garage, and the man behind the counter began reaching towards the cigarettes, asking as he did if I wanted 20 or 40 today. I paused, then replied, 'None.' There were no cigarettes in my pocket as I headed to the court – an unheard-of omission. I had lunch that day with a Major-smoking friend and refused the proffered cigarette to accompany my coffee. And that was it. I never smoked again. I just stopped cold. It was those two words – 'under control' – that had done it. I resented the implication so much that I showed my GP exactly how much control I could muster.

Of course, if you have an addictive personality, it will get channelled into something. Mine is now channelled into solitaire, which I play compulsively on my laptop every day. I've already mentioned my mother's predilection for alcohol, which was kept firmly in check by my father. But then, my father insisted on buying a Lotto ticket every week, even though he never won anything. I thought it was the silliest behaviour. I'd rather have given the money to charity. But there you have it; I think we all have something we cling on to. You just have to hope it's something benign rather than something malignant.

These self-realisations may sound minor, but they were the cornerstone of my court and how I conducted it. It's difficult to empathise with a defendant in a courtroom if you've never been one yourself. In this respect, I learned so much from John Lonergan, who was wondrously empathetic to the men he dealt with in Mountjoy Prison. John was a one-off who had a positive ripple effect on so many lives. But that's exactly why I enjoyed the District Court so much, because of the high level of involvement with the people who committed crimes. I relished the challenge of working with them and trying in some small way to advocate for change in their lives.

And thanks to my president who had sent me there, I had carte blanche to do whatever I liked in Kilmainham. I was in charge every time I sat into that chair. I set about putting into practice the lessons I was learning daily, and I worked to create a court that investigated each case from every point of view – victim, defendant, gardaí and Probation Service. The key lesson for me was that compassion and empathy had to be allied with knowledge, because that was the only way to achieve good judgments that, I hoped, would stand the test of time. For my part, I felt that my approach could be more about judging or more about understanding. I chose understanding.

CHAPTER 5

IF YOU DON'T GET IT FROM THE HORSE'S MOUTH, STOP LISTENING TO THE ASS WHO TOLD YOU

There are always at least two sides to every story. This becomes more and more evident as you get older and begin to see the grey areas with crystal clarity. In youth, it's much easier to be distracted by the black and the white and the choosing of sides, but age bestows the grey – in every way! – and that is, in fact, a gift. There are few pure truths in life, and it is helpful to understand that. There can be so much unseen, unheard, unnoticed, but it is in those quiet spaces that you'll often find the broadest version of the truth, encompassing its many facets. When I was on the bench, I learned that I had to be open to all elements of each story – the victim's story, the accused's story, the gardaí's story and the unspoken, between-the-lines story that was there in the courtroom if I took the time to listen to it. A good judge is a committed listener.

This comes back to the desire to understand, which to my mind is the best form of compassion. It is an act of compassion and empathy to listen attentively to what someone has to say. That's why I always tried to take the time to hear as many voices as possible, when the case allowed. If a not guilty plea was entered and the case went to a hearing, that presented a chance to dig deeper into the why behind what had occurred. When possible, I took that chance. The rewards of that kind of compassion and empathy can be huge: second chances and rebuilt lives. If it was in my power to do so, I wanted to help.

During my time in Kilmainham, which stretched from 1986 to 2002, there wasn't much in the way of help for victims – particularly not in my first decade on the bench there. Victim Support was in its infancy, as a concept as well as a practical aid. There are no victim impact statements in the District Court, and back then the victim cut a lonely figure because there weren't the support organisations that are doing such wonderful work now. The entire court set-up was geared around the accused person and their defence. That meant the criminals were the most real people in the room, hogging the spotlight. The victim was in the shadows, watching on, reduced to the role of spectator.

The hearings took place in the afternoon and when I entered the courtroom after lunch, I'd have a quick look around. I could tell immediately if the victim was present. It was invariably the face I didn't know, pale, looking anxious and uncomfortable in that setting. I'd be thinking, *Right, it's going to be a long afternoon.* It was clear they hadn't a clue about anything in the court or its proceedings. I could see them wondering if they should genuflect to me.

There was no call for me, as the judge, to talk to the victim, but I made a point of it whenever possible if an accused had suddenly decided to change the plea to guilty. A plea of not guilty ensured that the victim would be requested to take the stand, but a guilty plea excluded the necessity for this. However, I'd ask the prosecuting garda, 'Is the victim in court today?' even though I'd already spotted them. When the garda confirmed the victim was there, I would ask him to go over and invite them up into the dock to tell me their story. The majority of them agreed to do so, and I admired them for it because it wasn't easy to walk across the brown floor and climb the steps up into the witness box and speak out like that. Most times, it was the first time they'd seen the accused since the incident, and they were seated close by. It was terribly daunting. It was also often the first time the victim had publicly described what had happened to them, from their point of view. I felt it was extremely important to give them the chance to talk and to be heard.

One day, there was a tall, lanky chap in the dock who had stolen a car. I invited the woman who owned the car up to the box to speak. She came up, trembling with nerves, and told me she had mobility issues, so her car was her lifeline. The theft of the vehicle wasn't a simple inconvenience, it had caused her huge problems and distress because the car was adapted for her needs, and it gave her independence. After she finished speaking, I turned to the lanky chap and asked him, 'Do you understand the hurt and inconvenience you caused this lady?' He replied, 'Wha'?' Three times I asked, and three times he gave me that same monosyllabic answer. After that, I shook my head and said, 'Forget it. We are not on the same planet.' I sent him to prison. He wasn't ready to listen, which meant he wasn't ready to change.

There wasn't much I could do for victims, but this approach seemed a helpful one to me. When they stepped into the box, I'd tell them I was delighted to have them there, to put them at their ease. Then I'd ask for their version of the events, and I'd give them time to speak, letting them elaborate as they wished without hurrying them along. My job was to listen to the prosecuting garda, read the charge sheet and make a decision, and that was all. But in my book, that was totally wrong because that victim was still victimised. There was no restorative justice back then, but I felt that the opportunity to speak and to be heard might help in the recovery process. I hope it did. I'm only sorry that I wasn't able to do it more often.

After I retired, I was able to keep listening to victims, because in 2006 the wonderful and very caring Maeve Ryan of the National Crime Victims Helpline invited me to be the patron of this invaluable support service. I said that if I were to be a patron, I had to be a volunteer too and experience the frontline. I worked for them every Saturday from home, and I also did one weekday morning in the office, answering phones and listening to the stories of people who had been traumatised to one degree or another by a crime that had been visited upon them. I did that until 2019, when poor health intervened and I had to give up volunteering with them, although I'm still a patron. What I loved about it was that there were always young students among the volunteers, and that gladdened my heart. I was watching their empathy being stimulated and shaped, and I knew they'd have that for the rest of their lives and always offer a helping hand when they could. The sort of awareness they were building up from doing that work was so valuable – both for them as individuals and for society at large.

Over time as a judge, you learn to read the situation before you by listening to everything.

Remember: the judge cannot bone up on the cases or the law beforehand – we have to take each case as it comes and deal with it there and then to the best of our ability. I was always listening out for anything that could help me in reaching the best decision. In my early days in Kilmainham, there was a case involving a young man from a well-known criminal family. He had committed what was classed as a minor assault against his girlfriend – my recollection is that he had slapped her – and given his family background, many might have viewed it as an open-and-shut case. The young man was in the box, being asked about his behaviour towards his 'girlfriend', as he referred to her, when I happened to overhear a quiet remark from the prosecuting garda: 'He doesn't have a girlfriend.'

It might have been just a throwaway comment, but that snippet made me wonder, gave me pause. I got the Probation Service involved and put him on probation for 12 months. I felt so pleased when I later read the probation report. It noted that the young man was gay and going through a tough time as a result, and that his behaviour towards the girl in question had stemmed from the conflict and difficulty he was experiencing because of his sexuality. That was the last time I ever saw him. He got help from the Probation Service and didn't look back. I was very glad that I'd heard that quiet, off-the-cuff remark and caught the significance of it. It was just enough to plant a small seed of doubt in my head, and that made all the difference.

When a judge doesn't read a situation well, it can have disastrous consequences. There was a criminal, involved in the drugs trade, who applied for a taxi licence. The gardaí refused to grant it, so the man appealed that decision to the District Court. It came before a relatively new judge, who knew nothing of this man's past dealings with the gardaí or the court. This wasn't the judge's fault, of course, but it did mean that he wasn't taking in the whole situation before him. As a result, he awarded the licence, and the 'taxi driver' later harmed a female passenger. I often read things now on District Court decisions and find myself wondering if the judge is new to the bench because of what they haven't heard or noticed, and what they have subsequently decided. But as I said, it's not the judge's fault: it just takes time and experience to read each situation quickly and thoroughly.

The other thing that no one taught us as judges was how to read a Book of Evidence. We had to figure that one out for ourselves. The judge cannot discuss the Book with the gardaí, prosecution or defence, so it requires dedication and close attention to 'hear' everything it's telling you about the case. We see only the evidence presented in court, but the Book of Evidence can contain other important information. I used to read them very carefully, cover to cover, focusing fiercely on every line. I liked to read them in bed at night, like a good thriller, on the lookout for clues or telling details.

The point of reading the Book of Evidence was to weigh up the evidence, which was mainly witness statements in the District Court, and decide whether to send the case forward for a jury trial in the higher courts. When reading a Book, I would be on the alert for any missing links, any details that contradicted each other or didn't add up. It had to present a watertight argument that there was a case to answer. If, for any reason, I had felt the prosecution hadn't presented a convincing case, I would have been hesitant to send forward the case. But I have to say, in all my years on the bench I rarely came across anything like that. The gardaí must first submit the Book of Evidence to the DPP, which assesses it and sends it back if any inconsistencies are found, requesting additional, clarifying inform-ation or further evidence. That meant the DPP was on those details before the Book ever reached me. That's a very good fail-safe, because it means the gardaí are not solely responsible for securing the case – they have the legal backup and advice of the DPP. It also ensures the gardaí go that extra mile to ensure all angles are covered for a court of law. It's a good system.

The John Gilligan case back in my Bridewell days was a good example of a case that couldn't proceed because the Book of Evidence was incom-plete. The gardaí wanted to prosecute Gilligan for being in possession of 250 videotapes, but they could not prove who owned the tapes. That crucial piece of evidence was missing. As a result, the case could not be sent forward. The high level of certainty necessary to send a case forward simply wasn't there – no matter how sure the gardaí were that a crime had been committed. I've seen the utter frustration this can sometimes cause to the gardaí, and I feel for them, but it is important that any judgment is based on a high level of certainty, so that justice can be served.

The other thing I learned to listen to was what was not said. My finest moment on the bench, as far as I'm concerned, came from listening to the silent eloquence of body language. I look back on that judgment with pride and satisfaction, something I can't say about every decision I made. The case involved a priest, Fr Tony Walsh. He was known as The Singing Priest because he toured with the All Priests Show, performing an Elvis Presley tribute act. He was the hail-fellow-well-met type: gregarious, charming, good-looking. These attributes made him very dangerous because he could fool people easily – and he could groom innocent children.

Walsh was brought before me in Kilmainham on station bail in February 1995. If a person was arrested at night and taken to a garda station, they would give their details and be interviewed. If the gardaí were satisfied that this person would turn up in court the next day, they would grant bail. This was granted when the accused signed a document called a station bail, with no money paid over. However, if the gardaí weren't happy with the details supplied, or if a bench warrant already existed for the person in question, that person would be obliged to remain in custody and arrive at court in custody. At that point, it became the discretion of the District Court judge if bail was granted or not.

When Fr Tony Walsh appeared at Kilmainham, it was on a sexual offence charge. This was deeply shocking, because at that point sexual offences didn't occur in court very often, plus the Catholic Church was still very much in its ascendancy in Ireland. It was unprecedented to have a serving priest appear as a defendant. There still prevailed at that time a view that clerics were closer to God than the rest of us, so across the country there was near-disbelief and outrage that a priest could be suspected of and charged with one of the worst possible crimes: child abuse. Walsh's solicitor requested free legal aid, and I replied, 'Can you imagine the headlines? Definitely not.' I remanded the case to await the DPP's decision on which court the case would be heard in. I asked Walsh his plea, and he answered, 'Not guilty.' We set a date for a hearing.

On the day of the hearing, the court was very full. I was surprised by that – all I knew of Walsh at that point was this one allegation and his assertion that he wasn't guilty. I wasn't aware, then, of his reputation in the communities where he worked or the amount of people he had hurt and trauma-tised with his behaviour. Before me that day was a man of the cloth accused of a sexual offence he denied committing. It was an unusual situation – although Walsh wouldn't be the last man of the cloth to come before me for such crimes. The victim was in court for the hearing. He was a 12-year-old boy at the time of the alleged incident, now 13 years of age. The prosecution was arguing that the alleged incident had taken place at the Silver Granite pub in Upper Ballyfermot on the occasion of the victim's grandfather's funeral. The young boy took to the witness box to give his testimony. He was sitting to my right, slightly elevated. Walsh sat behind his solicitor and barrister, straight in front of me. The prosecution team were to the left of me.

I could not tell you one single thing about that child's appearance. As the prosecution, then the defence, put him through his evidence, I never once looked at him. I listened to him with every fibre of my being, but at the same time I never, ever took my eyes off Walsh. I watched him as intently as I listened to the boy. I was listening to Walsh's body language, noting everything about his demeanour. This wasn't a planned tactic on my part, it was simply my natural response to the scene unfolding before me. I felt so sorry for the young boy, having to give intimate, upsetting evidence in a crowded court like that. He was so very young, a child, and it must have been a nightmare for him. I heard his every word, but Walsh's body language spoke just as loudly, and I heard everything it said.

As I watched, I could see that the priest was taking absolute delight in listening to the incident as described in detail by the boy. The pleasure he was taking in listening to it being recounted was clear. I watched and I listened, and by the time the boy was finished speaking, there was no doubt in my mind that the man in front of me had committed this crime. He had convicted himself with his reaction to the boy's testimony.

The defence mounted its argument next, and it was very persuasive. That was largely because the key character witness, who provided a seemingly cast-iron alibi, was a prison officer. He told the court that he was with Walsh when the alleged incident had occurred, which meant the boy could not be telling the truth. Walsh himself took the stand as well. He told me that he had left the pub and gone with a pal – the prison officer – to look at a Mazda 626 he was thinking of buying. I told him that I had no interest in cars. He replied that this meant he could not have committed the act against the boy. If I hadn't listened so closely to Walsh's body language, his evidence and that of the prison officer might have swayed me to find in his favour. This was a powerful counterargument by two respected professionals. I shudder to think how easily it could have gone the other way. As it was, the priest's performance in the witness box did not change my mind, nor did the performance of his pal. I convicted Walsh and gave him a 12-month sentence. I accepted his brother as a bailsperson for an appeal. I was later told that the priest was seen that very night, after the hearing, in a pub in

Drumcondra, drinking – a toast to his conviction and 'escape', no doubt.

But he didn't escape. The complaints against Walsh mounted, and some time later he was back in court on similar offences. The DPP decided to send this case to the higher courts, which meant the compilation of a full Book of Evidence. That, again, came through me in Kilmainham, and I was pleased to pass him on to face the full rigours of a trial in the higher courts. Annoyingly, Walsh's appeal against my judgment of 12 months was not heard before his case reached the higher courts. A conviction is not recorded until all appeals have been exhausted, so he arrived there without any recorded convictions to his name.

Nonetheless, he was handed down a sentence of nine years for offences against two brothers. I remember reading that Book of Evidence and being deeply shocked. Walsh had been moved from Ballyfermot to a church in Westland Row, but he continued to visit his old turf. These two brothers were of particular interest to him, and he regularly collected them and brought them for visits in Westland Row. Unbeknown to their parents, who liked and trusted the friendly priest, Walsh had groomed these children and was sexually abusing them. This particular day, he brought them to Westland Row and up to his room. However, he was unexpectedly called to cover for another priest and say mass. While the two brothers waited for Walsh to return, they perused the books on his shelves. They picked one down and opened it – and out fell photos of naked young boys – boys they knew from Ballyfermot. They put the pictures back carefully and waited. I was never able to forget that sentence, or that image, of the two youngsters, groomed to obedience, awaiting their fate.

Much later, after I had retired and was chair of the Catholic Church Commission on Child Sexual Abuse, I went to a solicitor's office for a meeting, accompanied by a man working for the Catholic hierarchy. Before we began the meeting, the solicitor mentioned the Walsh case. He said to me, 'That was an inspired decision. How did you make it?' I was taken aback, and when I asked him how he knew about it, he told me that he had been in the courtroom that day. 'Where were you?' I asked. He said he was at the back of the room, in the press of onlookers. 'Well, that's the difference,' I said. 'I was up front, looking right at Tony Walsh while the victim gave his evidence, and that's how I knew what judgment to make on the case.' There must have been all sorts of interest in the case that day that I wasn't aware of, but it was very interesting to hear this assessment. Years later, after my 2020 appearance on *The Tommy Tiernan Show* on RTÉ television, I received a letter from a woman who told me that many friends of hers in Ballyfermot had been abused by Fr Tony Walsh. She thanked me for my decision that day and said it had helped so many, either by saving them from further abuse, or by helping them to report it and begin their recovery process. That was a shock, I can tell you. But I was delighted to hear it. My gut instinct had been right that day.

Perhaps the most difficult story to listen to with empathy and focused understanding is that of the accused. It would be easy to view them as being on a lower rung of the ladder, there only to be judged. However, I always saw my responsibility as a judge as being bigger than passing judgments. I believed I could also put in place the most helpful conditions for a person to change, if they were ready and willing to do so. If they weren't ready, prison was often the best judgment to make. But if there was a chance of getting through to them, of showing them the consequences of their actions in a manner that could convince them to discontinue that behaviour, then I was always ready to engage with that option via the Probation Service.

This was why I made it my modus operandi to talk to those accused, to engage with them on equal terms and to get the whole story of the crime straight from the horses' mouths, both the accused's and the victim's viewpoints, if possible. The accused is a person too, not an object in the dock. My own observation over the years was that if a judge didn't talk with the accused on this basis, they were more likely to give them a prison sentence. That might miss a vital opportunity to pull a person away from crime and the prison population, which, as I often say, is a win-win situation all round if you can facilitate it.

The first time I did this was, I think, with Helen Spellman. I first met her in the Bridewell in 1985. She was a young woman with a criminal record and a boyfriend in prison for murder. Helen's life was teetering on the brink, and she was in and out of the Bridewell Courthouse. I felt for this girl, who seemed so young and so lost. She didn't strike me as a hardened criminal – far from it. She was caught up in circumstances that were prompting her behaviour, but she was more than just her behaviour. Helen and I became friendly. I invited her to visit me at Kilmainham, and I'd take her out to lunch. We talked about her life, and I got a proper insight into how a life can spiral out of control. She described her chaotic background: four siblings, an alcoholic dad, a mother who turned to shoplifting to keep the family going. It was Helen's job to mind her siblings, and as a result she'd never had a full week at school. It was all too easy to fall in with a life of crime, most of it petty crime – though, of course, that can always lead to bigger things.

I enjoyed those lunches with Helen, and I hoped she enjoyed them too. Eventually we lost touch, but I thought about her often. Then, several years later, I was at a graduation ceremony at a drug treatment centre, and lo and behold, there was Helen. She was working as an addiction counsellor. Her life seemed to have come full circle. She was now helping others as she had once been helped. My old lunch companion was a force for good in the world, and that was wonderful to see.

Helen was one of the first people I met in the dock with whom I ended up becoming friends. She was a good person underneath the difficult circumstances, and she proved that in spades by turning her life around and choosing to work as a counsellor. It was people like Helen – and there were many – who convinced me that the listening and facilitating approach was the right one. It can work. And when compassion works, the dividends are huge.

Paul Mahon is another excellent example. Paul came to Kilmainham occasionally. He was always in the custody of prison officers, and his 'occasional' visits usually led to him being sent forward to a higher court and served with a custodial sentence. On one of the last occasions that he appeared in Kilmainham court, he was up on serious charges – for the umpteenth time. His charge sheets were both frightening and impressive. After the hearing, Paul was being escorted back to the prison van by two officers when he managed to get away from them and made a dash for it. He ran out of the courthouse in Kilmainham, sprinted across the road and down the hill, where he jumped over a wall – no doubt thinking he was home free. What he failed to realise was that on the other side of the wall was a circa 25ft drop down into the River Camac. He dropped into the water like a stone and was rearrested where he fell. It was then the prison officers discovered the knife hidden in his shoe.

That was in the 1990s, and Paul Mahon looked like a man whose life had hit the skids in a cul-de-sac. Where else was there for him to go after this? He was a seemingly hopeless drug addict, his life punctuated by serious crimes like armed robbery, arrests and prison spells, and then back out on to the streets to start the whole cycle again. I was actually terrified of him, he was that out of control, that beyond himself. Fast forward to 2018, and where is Paul Mahon? Sitting next to me on the set of *The Late Late Show*, telling Ryan Tubridy about his life of crime and addiction, his new life of sobriety and his friendship with me. The man I thought would likely die on the streets is now drug-free and a contributing member of society. We meet for lunch whenever we can, and I marvel at the chapters of his story that have been added on as a result of him choosing a different path. No one was able to force him on to that path, but we in the Courts and Probation services just kept holding up the sign that pointed that way.

As Paul himself says, 'Eventually there came a time when I said, "I can't take this anymore."' He had to arrive at the desire to fix his drug problem by himself, and then he was ready to listen and to act. He went into Tiglin, an addiction treatment centre, and has never looked back. I went to a graduation at that treatment centre, not knowing Paul had mended his ways, and there he was, sober and ready to go out into the world again. He spotted me in the crowd and asked the chairman, 'What's that woman doing here?' I was used to that reaction from former prisoners! We ended up talking at length that day, and we've been friends ever since. Paul is living proof that with the right supports and understanding, people can change, no matter how far gone they seem to be. When that transformation occurs, it gives me great pleasure. I attend many graduations at treatment centres, and my face aches from smiling afterwards, but seeing those people emerge, renewed, I can't stop beaming for joy. They were lost, and they are found.

It takes an army of people to help a person effect this kind of transformation, and to my mind it all starts with listening. That simple act of understanding can be a powerful agent for change. In the court as in life, we are a better society if we extend a helping hand when it can work. If it's not the right time and it won't work, fine, prison sentence. But when that moment that Paul Mahon described – that moment when the person is tired of it all, weary with their own self – arrives, that's when it's possible to turn empathy into positive action.

CHAPTER 6

ALWAYS HAND BACK THE CONDOMS...
OR A SENSE OF HUMOUR IS VITAL

One of the things I really enjoyed about the District Court was that my character and sense of humour could play a role in the proceedings. It was a rough-and-tumble court, noisy, bustling, with frequent bursts of laughter. That suited me just fine. There was no hushed reverence or playing holier-than-thou. I could be myself and administer justice just as well. I didn't have to play the part of 'Judge' with a capital J. I simply did my own thing in my own way and made the best decisions I could make in the circumstances.

I'm often asked about the relentless human tragedy that poured through the court and how I coped with it. Well, I felt the gardaí had it the worst on that score. They were really on the frontlines, out on the streets, dealing with entirely unpredictable situations and people. I felt for them greatly and was very glad not to be among their number. Much easier to sit in the safety of a courtroom, when the incident is long over and the offending person is constrained and calm. That said, it was important to have coping mechanisms, because the days were filled with so much and all kinds of sadness. I'm not quite sure how, but I managed to leave that sadness behind me each day. I had my father living with me at the time, and he never wanted to know about that side of my life, so I left it outside the front door when I came home. My greatest coping mechanisms were playing golf and watching sports on television. And *Crimecall* – I watched that religiously, and still do.

At work, we all used humour to manage the wretchedness and to do our jobs well. I enjoyed the witty gallows humour of the gardaí. It was a huge part of the reason why I enjoyed socialising with them so much. They faced such difficult circumstances day in, day out, but they joked and laughed together and got through. It was the same for solicitors, barristers and judges. You couldn't be part of the criminal justice system and not have a sense of humour, to be honest. It was definitely an effective coping mechanism.

I remember watching a documentary on Mountjoy Prison. It was very insightful, and one inmate, in particular, made me smile. Talking about his daily routine, he intoned mournfully that it was 'fucken cornflakes for breakfast, fucken cornflakes for lunch, fucken cornflakes for tea'. A few weeks later, I was sitting in a night court. The gardaí brought in an accused in custody, and I looked up to see this selfsame inmate standing before me. 'Oh look,' I said, 'it's Fucken Cornflakes.' The barrister nearly fell down in shock. Eyes wide, he looked at me and said in his plummy voice, 'I'm sorry, Judge?' That amused me no end. His shock was hilarious.

I've already recounted the story from my early days when condoms were handed up as evidence, and I didn't know that I was supposed to hand them back until the barrister inquired mischievously if I was holding on to them because I'd be needing them. That was my first lesson in court humour, and it showed me that there was no need to be po-faced to do the job properly. When barristers had to make their way to Kilmainham, they were often a bit thrown by the chaotic nature of things there. There was a young barrister who came into the court one day and asked one of the gardaí, 'Where is the robing room?' His face was a picture when everyone burst out laughing. There are no robes in the District Court, and definitely no robing room. I also recall another young barrister who attended one day, defending a chap brought in by Garda Flynn. As we tried to conduct our business, the chap was roaring from the cells about 'Perjuror Flynn' and 'Lesbian Hussey'. I laughed to myself as I watched the barrister's neck get redder and redder in embarrassment. He wouldn't have heard the likes of that in the Four Courts.

I could be a bit brazen as well, when the mood took me. On his final visit to my court, I was remanding Christy Kinahan for the Book of Evidence to be prepared and I said to him, 'Come back next Thursday.' He told me that he couldn't come to court that day because he was working. I peered at him over my glasses. 'You? At what?' He replied, 'I'm a carpenter, Judge.' I gave him a sharp look and said, 'I wouldn't want you around my house.' I could see the gardaí stifling smiles at that one.

Whenever a defendant requested free legal aid, I was always quick to retort, 'Nothing is free. Someone is paying for it. Me!' The crime I hated hearing the most was social welfare fraud. There was nothing to be done, which irked me. Usually, the deceit had been going on for years before it was finally noticed, and the sum owed would be far beyond the fraudster's means. There was no point sending them to prison, since that just added to the burden on the taxpayer. And there was no point in community service for this type of crime, either. All I could do was hand down a suspended sentence. It was a complete waste of everyone's time, and that really annoyed me.

There was one man brought before me with a typical case. He had been royally defrauding the Revenue, claiming social welfare for himself and on behalf of his absent brother while also working a full-time job. He was coining it in and had been for years. I thought it was an extraordinary mentality that could lead a person to do that. The prosecuting detective informed me that the man was 'paying it back at one pound a week'. I looked at this person wasting my time and said, 'Well, I hope you have a very long life!'

I was well known for having a long and vicious memory, and criminals hated me for it. I volunteered to do night courts because I lived not far from the Bridewell, where they were held. Back then, if a person was arrested under certain Acts, they had to be charged or released within twelve hours. The day courts ended at 4.30 p.m., so the gardaí could be in a bind if the timeframe went against them. Hence the need for night courts. Some District Court judges refused to participate in them, but I was always happy to do so. I don't think we received any extra payment for it – maybe that was why many of my colleagues weren't keen. It was easy enough work, though – I'd get a phone call to say I was needed, the gardaí would turn up in a patrol car to collect me and drive me to the Bridewell, and then they'd drive me home again afterwards. I knew they needed that service, so I always made myself available for it.

There was laughter in court one night when they brought in the accused in question, and the court registrar called out his name. I took one look at him and said, 'That's not his name. That's his brother.' The accused looked up, astounded, then shook his head. 'Fuck it, I didn't know you'd be on tonight,' he said. That memory of mine was an effective weapon – and I miss it greatly now that age has blunted it.

I also remember being driven home in the patrol car one night, after a night court session, and seeing my neighbour – resplendent in a pink suit and spiky high heels, sashaying down the street without a care in the world, confident and fierce. This man was years ahead of his time, and I admired him hugely. The two uniformed gardaí accompanying me were agog at the sight of him. I smiled to see my garda escorts wide-eyed and wide-mouthed, staring at this vision in pink. I also smiled because I loved his attitude – that man was amazing.

I was often called at night to sign warrants when the gardaí needed to search a premises. For example, they had to have a warrant to enter a brothel, which was a pretty regular occurrence as part of their campaign against the illegal sex trade. They knew I was approachable and willing to help, so I'd get a call, the patrol car would arrive and I'd gladly check and sign the warrant so they could go and investigate. Those cases usually ended up in the Circuit Court, but they would first come through Kilmainham, for remand and the preparation of a Book of Evidence. One day, one of my colleagues on the bench asked me how I managed to get all these brothel cases. I noted his interest and, much to his embarrassment, I told him I'd give him their cards!

The gardaí appreciated the fact that I was ready to help, and I became great friends with many of them over the years. I would join them on nights out or on weekend golf trips. We never talked work on these occasions – we all needed a break from that. I remember a Christmas night out in a pub in Bluebell, and the gardaí were all sending over drinks to me at the bar. The barman kept adding to a long line of drinks set out along the bar and intended for me. I kept surreptitiously pouring them into any receptacle I could find. The flowerpots were well watered that night, although I'd say the poor plants never recovered. But there were so many drinks sent over, it got to the point that I had to quietly ask the barman to get rid of them. At 3 a.m. I was getting ready to leave and I took out my car keys. The superintendent stared at me in shock. 'Are you okay to drive, Judge?' he asked. I had to laugh – he thought I'd downed the entire line of drinks. I think I'd have been face down on the floor if I hadn't consigned them to the flowerpots.

Not all the gardaí were clued in, though. In 1987 or thereabouts, the superintendent at Kevin Street Garda Station came to the court to speak to me. He told me that the National Boxing Stadium wasn't doing well and asked if I could help. He knew I loved sport, and he was thinking that my presence at matches would raise the stadium's profile. My first instinct was, *I love sport, but not boxing, so no, thank you.* But then I thought, *Hang on, I'm working in a crime-ridden area, and boxing could help to prevent crime by keeping youngsters on the straight and narrow, so why not?* I said I'd help, and I've been attending fights at the National Stadium every year since then.

On one occasion, after a boxing match, a garda sergeant who was visiting Dublin from Donegal offered to walk me to my car since it was a dark night. Outside the National Stadium, we encountered two young uniformed gardaí on foot patrol. The sergeant asked them to show 'the judge to their car', and one of the young men replied, 'Where is he?' Quite. We got that sorted, and they walked with me. I asked how long they'd been at the Kevin Street station, and they said 18 months. The next thing, a little stocky fella, of the local low-level thug fraternity, jumps out from behind my car and says, 'Gillian, I was just minding your car for you.' I gave the young garda a look. *See, I was thinking, you're 18 months on the job, and you've no idea who I am, while this fella could probably recite my CV.* I'm still chairman of the Disciplinary Committee of the National Stadium – no harm, no foul.

In terms of defendants, there were a few who made a distinct impression. One, in particular, was the man in the dock who fired an apple at me. It whistled past the side of my head. It wasn't even a half-eaten apple – he fired the whole thing at me, and with forceful intent. I didn't flinch or move in my seat. I just looked at him and said as nonchalantly as I could, 'That was a poor shot.' There was much laughter around the court at that. However, when the hearing ended, and I got up to leave, I turned to look at where the apple had hit and realised I'd had a very close call. The apple had exploded on impact and was splattered all across the wall. If it had hit me, it would have been a hell of a smack. I was glad I'd handled it with humour and laughed it off, but I wasn't laughing when I saw the state of the wall. It would have clocked me if he'd been on target.

Another defendant who stood out was a young woman called Samantha Blandford Hutton. Her mother owned the very successful Tuthills newsagents, but Samantha had chosen a different profession. She ran what was described as one of the best brothels in Dublin, and in fact she would go on to become the first person in Ireland to be convicted of organised prostitution. When I saw her in the dock in Kilmainham for the second time – the first time was on a shoplifting charge and I handed her a suspended sentence – she was accused, along with her brother and his girlfriend, of controlling and organising prostitution, managing a brothel and living off the earnings of prostitution. All three of them were wearing identical long black cloaks with red satin lining and the two women completed their ensemble with black evening gloves. There were three other people similarly dressed in the back area of the court, and when their case was finished all six walked out to a waiting press, frantic to get pictures of them. It was a strange display, and I couldn't make head nor tail of it. Were they doing it for attention? Or was it to make themselves look intimidating? I confess, that sort of behaviour is so far beyond my own mental bailiwick that I was at a loss to understand its purpose, but it was certainly eye-catching.

I was in the witness box myself once, as a witness in a defamation case for a colleague. It was heard in the High Court, and I was cross-examined by Michael McDowell SC. He was being pretty hard on me, and the things he was saying weren't adding up. I was perplexed. Then I realised what was happening: he had mistaken me for my relative, who was a government minister. I looked at him and said, 'Excuse me, I'm not Gemma Hussey.' The consternation! The judge ordered him to apologise to me, which he did. That made me smile.

The cells at Kilmainham had previously been under the courtroom, but when they built new ones, they positioned them down a corridor beside the courtroom, along the handiest exit route. I took that quick way out every day at lunchtime. As I trotted past the cells, those inside would be thundering abuse at me, every name under the sun, scurrilous allegations about my sexuality and predilections, all couched in the most colourful language imaginable. It didn't bother me a bit. I'd always cheerily call back, 'I'm off out, lads, to enjoy my lunch.' I was amused to hear that any other judge who sat in my court refused to use that exit. I was the only one to run the gauntlet. I did it every day, happily, and it didn't cost me a thought. I rather enjoyed the outlandish comments the prisoners came up with to fling at me – very inventive, I thought.

I remember when John Lonergan invited me to view the newly built Dóchas Centre, the prison for women at Mountjoy. It was splendid, and I said to John, 'I'd like to be put in here, it's so lovely. I think I might issue myself a warrant.' That made him laugh.

There was a case that came before me – first in the Bridewell, and then again while I was in Kilmainham. The plaintiffs were the street traders of Henry Street. They were a famous part of Dublin lore and landscape, but a dispute with Dublin Corporation threatened their livelihood. The Corporation asserted that the traders were not compliant with the statutory provisions of the Casual Trading Act 1980. As a result, the Corporation was refusing to grant licences to trade. The case came up in the Bridewell. I sent a case stated to the High Court, and by the time it came back to the Bridewell, I was sitting in Kilmainham. Therefore, I had to return to the Bridewell for one day to hear the case and pass judgment.

We conducted the hearing and, based on the legal advice issued by the High Court, I struck out the case against the traders. The court erupted as all the traders were present and they were wildly happy with this long-awaited outcome. Afterwards, the registrar, who knew me of old, suggested we repair to The Legal Eagle pub for a catch-up over a drink.

We opened the door of the pub, and my entrance was marked by a deafening, raucous cheer. All of the traders were in there, toasting their victory, and the excitement was at fever pitch. It seemed that the entire pub wanted to buy me a drink. It was a lovely scene of pure joy and great fun.

That wasn't the end of the matter, though. The Dublin City Business Association (DCBA) wrote to the president of the District Court to complain about me and my decision. They sent the letter to two senior members of An Garda as well. The president's secretary showed me the letter. I can't recall the exact contents now, but it was along the lines of 'How dare she', and I think they wanted me off the bench. I laughed at it, but the secretary looked at me askance and said it was actionable. That made me think. I went to my solicitor, who agreed it was actionable and that we should proceed on it. The DCBA had a plethora of members – the big stores like Arnotts and Brown Thomas among many others – and they all had to be sued as part of the proceedings. It was a magnificent work of art by the time the court proceedings were ready to issue. As it was, they offered me a settlement, and I took it. End of case.

I've seen this same humorous approach among the probation officers and the many ancillary court workers as well. There's a shared, unspoken understanding that it's necessary to leaven the sorrow. It's also very much in evidence in the area of drug addiction treatment. I have been heavily involved with centres like Tiglin for many, many years, and I'm always struck by the wit and humour of the staff and the residents. They have seen and experienced so many awful things, but they are the warmest people you could ever meet. A particular friend of mine is Aubrey McCarthy, founder of Tiglin and all-round powerhouse. Aubrey is an exceptional individual, a holy terror, and I love him to bits. I marvel at what he has achieved and all that he continues to do. He is rude but deeply effective!

Aubrey makes me laugh by always introducing me as 'Gillian, whom I met on Tinder'. I end up in all sorts of places when I'm with him. A few years ago, when I was 81, I found myself out in the city centre with Aubrey at 10.30 p.m. We had attended a fundraising event for St James's Camino, a drug addiction centre of which I am patron, but Aubrey embarked on a detour so he could visit a soup kitchen on O'Connell Street. So there I was, parked in Talbot Street, in the darkness, walking up to a soup kitchen outside Clerys. I was thinking, *This is a fine thing for a woman my age to be doing, out in the dark at all hours.* But that wouldn't faze Aubrey. He is never not doing good for someone, that's just who he is. But I had to laugh when a shout went up. 'Howya, Gillian, you gave me my first three sentences!' This was said with cheerful candour. I went over and sure enough, there was a repeat offender from my Kilmainham days. He had turned his life around and was now helping others further back down the road than him. It was a wonderful moment, and I treasured it.

It was people like Aubrey and the many gardaí, probation officers and legal colleagues who made my work so gratifying, even in the face of tough stories of loss, hardship and deprivation. They brought the humanity to court every day, which buoyed us all up. The barristers were so quick with a witty phrase and the gardaí with their dark humour, and I enjoyed all of it. Those bursts of laughter in court – even when provoked by a near-miss with an apple missile – told us all that there was more to life than what we were dealing with inside those four walls. That was a necessary and welcome reminder.

Sometimes, my work followed me to other, unexpected places, and that could create interesting juxtapositions. My uncle, Anthony Forrest Hussey, who was my mentor in the legal profession, was buried in Shanganagh Cemetery in Dublin in the 1990s. The priest officiating at the ceremony was a former legal aid solicitor whom I had met in my court when he was plying his former profession – that was one coincidence. We walked in solemn procession through the cemetery, coming to a stop at my uncle's final resting place. As the prayers were intoned and the hymns sung, my eyes kept being drawn to a large, monumental headstone nearby. When I noticed the family name, I had to suppress a smile. After the service, I went up to the priest and said to him, 'I just have to tell you this story because I know my uncle would be laughing to see where he was put!'

The name on the monument was that of a family who lived on the Belgard Road in Tallaght. The father was a sneaky individual, and his sons also ended up in my court. One day, one of the sons failed to appear, and I issued a bench warrant. The gardaí located him in Enniskerry, with a knife in his pocket. I immediately gave him a custodial sentence. I was later told by the gardaí that one of the women in the family had put a curse on me. I don't know what exactly that curse was, but I'm still alive at any rate. And now there they were, looking down on my uncle's grave from their elevated height. Talk about death being the leveller – it made me laugh, even as I said farewell to the uncle I had loved so dearly. And that's the thing about humour, I suppose – it shoots light through even the deepest darkness. We all need that.

CHAPTER 7

THE COURT IS A NETWORK HUB,
NOT A TERMINUS

There are different ways to view a court and its purpose within society. If you are there as a victim, naturally you want to feel that justice has been delivered and that the guilty party receives a commensurate punishment. If you are there as an accused, well, I'm not always sure what they are thinking, but I imagine they are either hoping to get off even if they are guilty or that the judge won't be too harsh, that justice will come with leniency and maybe even understanding. As for the rest of us, those who are facilitating the hearing and the justice to follow, I think we need to take a much wider view of what the court is and what it can achieve.

Over the course of my career on the bench, I have become convinced that the court isn't simply an end point for criminals, the last stop for the justice bus. It can be a network hub where experts join together to deliver justice for the victim, of course, but also to find out the best way of working with the guilty party and, ideally, to pull them off the path they are on and get them on to a new one. I see it as being about much more than the judgment. While that it is extremely important for all concerned, the judge can have a greater responsibility and a greater impact. This was why, from day one, I had an excellent relationship with both An Garda and the Probation Service. I saw them as skilled co-workers whose help I needed in order to do my job properly. In a very real way, the probation officers and the gardaí were the backbone of my court and of my judgments.

It takes a whole team of people working together to secure justice, that's the truth of the matter. People see the judge sitting up on high and think that is where justice resides. And it is in the District Court, in the sense that the judge must consider the case and deliver the judgment, so justice ultimately rests with them. However, I think much depends on how the judge wields that responsibility. You can choose to be an island, set apart, trusting your own thoughts alone. But that wouldn't be for me. I preferred to see justice as a network of many branches, with my court one part of it. If you truly want to help those who have committed crimes, you must reach out and start connecting these branches, so that they can avail of the help they need. It might not work. I know that first-hand because I've seen it happen. I've seen the opportunity refused and lost. That's life. But I never let that dampen my desire to keep trying. I knew, at the same time, that it could work and that it often did work.

It absolutely astounded me that many of my colleagues never used the Probation Service. For me, it was an invaluable source of information and insight. I simply could not have conducted my court without the input of the probation officers. Perhaps the lack of training was partly to blame.

We judges received no training in the role of the Probation Service or how to use it. Like everything else back then, it was a case of feeling your way in the dark until you found the light switch. And certainly, I had colleagues who never had that light-bulb moment. They steadfastly ignored the Probation Service and what it could do. Since it was at the judge's discretion to call them in or not, this was never challenged or questioned. I couldn't understand their position at all. To my mind, it's very hard to sit there, look at someone and make an assessment on the bare facts of the instant case. And if you don't hear the victim's side, which can often be the case, you are hearing only one side of the story as well. The Probation Service offered a vital way of exploring alternatives.

Once I had embarked on the course of talking to the defendants as much as possible, I knew that the Probation Service offered me a way of having an effective dialogue with them. In any case, some part of the judgment is based on an assessment of character. As the judge, you are compiling a broad picture of this person and this crime. I had the bones of the matter before me – the prosecution's narrative of what had occurred, the defence's narrative, the plea and perhaps a Book of Evidence. But if I asked for a probation report, a probation officer would visit that person at home, talk to them and assess their situation, and suddenly I could see so much more. That fleshed out the story with proper detail and real colour, and it moved all of us in the court beyond that single moment in that person's life when they committed the criminal act. I was always well aware that the victim could also often be frozen in that moment, requiring the court's help to move on by feeling that justice had been served, which hopefully brought them some sense of closure. However, I believed that as the non-involved, overseeing party, my own view had to be broader, and that I had to do what I could at a societal level, not simply at an individual level.

People often see judges as all-powerful – and, unfortunately, some judges also see themselves that way. I remember a woman in my court. She was at the end of her tether with her son, and she cried out to me, 'You're very powerful. Do something.' That woman came from a block of flats in Dublin 8 and had a tough, hard life. She was watching her son sink lower and lower, and her heart was broken. I often had mothers in my court, pleading for help, but I didn't have the power they thought I had. A judge has jurisdiction with borders, and with it comes responsibility. I had to respect the limits of my office. But I also understood that I could extend those borders and make that power more effective by using it as part of a network and working in tandem with An Garda and the probation officers.

The probation report was a very helpful tool. If I requested a report for an accused, I usually did so for one of two reasons – or both. First, it sometimes gave them a taste of incarceration. It took a week or so for the report to be prepared, and in that time the accused remained in custody, seeing what life looked like through the bars of a cell. There was no harm in that. Second, the report would give me a map of their life, charting all their previous charges up to this point (which were also given by the garda in court), their early life and education, and the probation officer's observations from the home visit, which were often crucial. It gave me a much better notion of the reasons behind their behaviour, which might in turn show me how best to intervene and hopefully help them to stop the behaviour that had landed them in court. The report and the inter-action with the Probation Service were the means by which I could give them a second chance, if that looked like a viable alternative to prison.

I admired the probation officers immensely. Like the gardaí, they had an extremely challenging job to do, and they did it with a sense of vocation and dedication that was inspiring. They did so much more than their work for the court. They brought me to see community service projects, for example, and that was a wonderful experience. I got to see fellas in a setting that was not a courtroom, and their pride and sense of purpose in the work they were doing was obvious. It was a completely other side to their characters. It gave them a sense of self-worth, a sense of being useful and good at something. Seeing that written on their faces always gave me huge pleasure. It bestowed on them an alternative viewpoint on their lives, one that they hadn't been able to see before. I know that young people today say, 'If you can't see it, you can't be it', and there's so much truth in that. These young men and women had often seen only crime, alcoholism and drugs – and people lost to those things. But once these services and projects opened the curtains and showed them what was beyond their own front door, it was like they were cured of life-blindness. It opened up the world to them.

It's like my friendship with probation officer Liz O'Donoghue – she's still a friend today and we meet up to drink coffee and reminisce, now that we're both retired. As I described earlier, Liz brought me on visits to certain houses in Dublin 10, giving me a direct insight into upbringings and family lives that were so markedly different from my own. I couldn't have pictured that without going there and seeing it for myself. The legal profession is stuffed with middle-class, privileged people who often have very nice, comfortable backgrounds. I'm one of them. But I think that puts the onus on us to find out more, to get out there and see what life is like for others before we pass judgment on their actions.

I had a funny and touching encounter recently. I was in my local Homebase store, and a salesperson wanted to talk to me about solar panels. I wasn't in a rush, so I stopped and listened to the spiel. At the end of it, I made an appointment for a representative of the company to call to my house to discuss it further. Before the appointment, I received a phone call from the company's office in Northern Ireland. The girl on the other end asked, 'Are you *Judge* Gillian Hussey?' I said I was. She turned out to be the daughter of a woman in Ballyfermot whose house I had visited. That woman was trying to cope with an alcoholic husband and two drug-addicted sons. I had sat in her home and talked to her. There was a little girl, a toddler, running around our feet as we chatted. The girl talking to me now was that child. She said to me, 'You knew my mother and my two brothers. I'm sending our top man down to you.' We had a lovely chat. Her mother had since died, but she had at least got her daughter out of that scene in Ballyfermot and into a good job. In those circumstances, that was an impressive achievement.

Liz was an incredible probation officer, totally committed to helping whenever and wherever she could, and clocking up hours of unpaid extra work in the process. In 1988 she set up We Have A Dream (WHAD), which was one of the best youth diversion projects I've ever seen. There was a group of young teenage fellas in Ballyfermot who were getting out of hand. Most of them hadn't yet faced charges in court, but they all looked to be heading that way. Some, I would have seen in my chamber for a talking-to, in a bid to get them to change their ways. They seemed to be on a slippery slope, however, and Liz decided to do something to help them. Off her own bat, she asked me, local priest Fr Denis Laverty, the chief superintendent of the district Michael Carolan and some local business owners to support her initiative. We all agreed. Liz arranged for the lads to work for Mooney's Car Sales, washing the forecourt every Saturday. They were not paid for this work – instead, Liz asked Mooney's to pay them in kind by giving the group a minibus in the summer to go on a trip. So those boys had to work towards an end goal rather than an immediate reward. They did it, though.

Come the summer, Superintendent John Courtney did all the paperwork to get them passports. The boys were all in their mid- to late teens, but none of them had ever been further than Dún Laoghaire. They piled into the van, with Liz and a male youth worker to chaperone them. That youth worker was another incredible person: after a string of convictions in his own youth, he had turned his life around and was now dedicated to helping others. He was able to speak to those boys in their language, and to show them that there were other paths through life than crime.

Well, off they went in their minibus, earned through their own hard work, and I had a lump in my throat as we waved them off. They went on a road trip in France, another chance to see far beyond their own front doors and limited expectations. And it proved to be a huge success. Most of them got out of crime after that experience. One of them came from a big crime family, and you wouldn't have had much hope for him escaping it, but escape he did, thanks to WHAD. That project dreamed up by Liz gave so much back to the community and generated such hope. I served as chair of WHAD from 1988 until my retirement in 2002, and it was hugely gratifying to be part of such a dynamic group. About three years after Liz set it up, the Probation Service came on board and brought it under its remit and funding, and I'm glad to say WHAD is still going strong to this day.

When I retired from the WHAD board, there was a get-together, and I was presented with a beautiful Waterford Crystal lamp. Unbeknown to the young chap who was presenting it to me, the lamp was in two parts. As he ceremoniously handed it over to me, one half came away and slipped from his hand. There was a gasp around the room as the crystal piece headed for the floor, but I managed to catch it before it got there. My reflexes were top-notch back then.

Another project I was very involved in was the Meath Street Activity Company (MSAC), now called the Meath Street Youth Activity Company (MSYAC), and I'm still a member of the board to this day. In my early days in Kilmainham, MSAC's chairperson Marie Stanley invited me to their awards ceremony. This was an ingenious event whereby they contacted all the schools in Dublin 8 and invited them to nominate pupils in various categories. They weren't your run-of-the-mill academic categories but included things like 'Most helpful to their grandparents', as well as achieve-ments in sport, music and other areas. These were children who might not ever win an academic award, but it meant so much to them to have their achievements recognised and honoured in this way. I had a wonderful evening at the ceremony, and I've been attending it annually ever since. MSYAC also organises weekly activities for the children, teaching them things like music, computers and drama. The company is run on a voluntary basis by the most wonderful bunch of people.

Marie Stanley is no longer involved in MSYAC due to ill health, but I will always have the highest admiration for her. Now the centre has an equally dedicated chair in Noel Fleming, who runs a bakery on Meath Street and is very kind-hearted and driven. There are kids I didn't see in my court thanks to WHAD – I saw their parents, but I didn't see them. I've been at MSYAC award ceremonies and received a knowing nod or wink from the audience, and it's a proud daddy who knows me professionally!

It is also the case that suicide rates are extremely high in these areas, and projects like those described above can help to provide a lifeline to young people. In recent years, I went to a coffee morning organised by MSYAC in league with a suicide awareness group. A group of gorgeous young women, all in their late teens or early twenties, caught my eye. They were standing together, talking, and their demeanour struck me – it seemed beyond their young years. When I was leaving, I stopped to thank them for being there and asked if any of them had been personally affected by suicide. They all nodded. It was just as I had suspected. Suicide was rampant in Dublin 8 at the time. That's why the work of probation officers, WHAD and MSYAC is so vitally important. If they didn't do it, there would be precious little help and support for these areas.

In terms of my court, I couldn't overstate the importance of the probation officers and their input on my judgments. And I still feel that is the best approach – to go beyond the crime to the causes that led to it. People often forget just how huge a role is played by mental health in crime, and you'd never uncover that if you didn't talk to the accused and find out what led to their actions. There isn't enough emphasis on that, in my opinion.

I also see a difference now in the set-up of the Probation Service, and they are not all welcome changes. After I retired, for example, I sat on a panel for interviewing potential new candidates for the Service. After one particular candidate had completed her interview and left the room, I said simply, 'I wouldn't like to see her in my court. There is a complete lack of empathy there.' The probation officers on the panel smiled and said, 'That's exactly why you're here'. The officers I had worked with were extraordinary people, with a passion for helping others in strange or sad circumstances. They had a common cause and huge empathy, which flowed through all of their work and initiatives. They went to visit homes gladly and prepared detailed reports on what they found there. Of course, there are many excellent people still in the Probation Service, but I think the focus is more office-based now, and that means losing vital information: those things you can learn only through a home visit. There are things that simply cannot be deciphered from a desk in an office. That level of empathy, of insight and of common humanity is necessary to be a really good probation officer, so it's worrying to see signs of it ebbing away in society. The pandemic has emphatically not helped this situation either, making engagement even more difficult.

I remember working with Joe Duffy when he was a probation officer in Ballyfermot, long before his current career as an RTÉ broadcaster. He was a great officer in his time, and we undertook several projects together. I retired on a Friday, and on the Monday, Joe and I had a great chat on the radio about the courts and the role of probation officers. It's funny, you often hear people groaning about Joe Duffy, declaring that they never listen to his daily phone-in show, *Liveline*, but I admire him for using his skills in this way. He gives a voice to the silenced in society and is often a last resort for those perhaps unable to fend for themselves. Joe has that skill of listening well, and it allows him to connect with people and give them a platform. I've always thought that he's in his right place in the world, at RTÉ. He was a wonderful probation officer, but the empathy that brought him to that job links perfectly with what he does now and allows him to do it so well. It's that same dedication to helping that I so admired in all the officers I worked with through my court – and I hope it's something we never lose in society, for then we'd all be the poorer.

I owe a great debt of gratitude to many probation officers, both men and women. They saw my innocence, but they also saw my willingness to learn, and they jumped at the chance to work with me and educate me. I found out that it worked both ways after I did an interview on television with Tommy Tiernan. Afterwards, I received a card from a 92-year-old former probation officer, who told me that she and her colleagues valued that fact that I had valued them. To my mind, that equality and respect between me, the officers and the gardaí created a more dynamic court, one that could be flexible and seek out justice in the best solutions for everyone. That network was invigorating for all of us, and it was sometimes very successful as well.

In terms of the gardaí, they were also very proactive in establishing youth diversion programmes, to try to reach out to the youngsters before they began to commit crimes. Kilmainham didn't deal with juvenile criminals – that is, those under 18 years of age – but I was always very interested in learning about those programmes. I hoped they would have a knock-on effect in my court by ensuring there would be absences by virtue of crimes *not* committed as a result. The gardaí who worked as juvenile liaison officers (JLOs) earned as much respect from me as the probation officers, and for similar reasons: because they had depths of empathy and understanding that were just incredible. I wish I knew what makes a good people person of that nature, but I don't – I just know they are different. I remember talking to a garda at a conference once. He had just become a JLO, so I asked him how it was going and what he would have done if he hadn't liked the work. He said without hesitation, 'I would have transferred immediately.' I loved that answer: honest and practical, and it meant he did love the job.

It was a well-known fact that I had a great relationship with the gardaí, but not everyone thought it was a good thing, as suggested by the odd snide remark muttered by a solicitor or barrister. But really, they didn't have the nerve to challenge me directly on it. As far as I was concerned, the gardaí were a key part of my education, just like the probation officers, and they taught me so much. There was mutual respect there, and I think my work benefited hugely from it. They also looked out for me and proved to be good friends over the years. I remember laughing one time when I had sold my car and just started driving my brand-new one. A garda came up to me in Kilmainham and said, 'Why the hell didn't you tell us about your new car? We chased the old one all over Dame Street last night.' And another night, in the late 1980s, I went to collect my son Ronan from the city centre. I parked off Pearse Street to wait for him, listening to the radio to pass the time. Next thing, a car sidles up beside mine and a detective peers out at me. 'What are you doing here?' he asked, astounded that it was me.

I also appreciated that they always looked out for me beyond the doors of the courtroom. If ever things got difficult with any case, I'd know the gardaí were keeping a discreet but close eye. There was one such occasion when a woman was murdered in the Dublin Mountains, and it was rumoured that the murderer was at large in Dublin 8. I wasn't the type to be spooked, but it was an odd feeling that there might be a menacing presence nearby, one that was capable of murder. I didn't wish to be publicly accompanied, and the gardaí were quietly aware of this, but I would notice an unmarked car following me to work and back home afterwards. This wasn't a policy or anything like that – it was simply individual, decent gardaí who added watching out for judges like me to their busy rosters. They did it from their own sense of duty, and they also managed to do it without being in any way obvious. As I said, I greatly appreciated it.

That behaviour typified the caring side of An Garda that you can see in spades in their youth work. I've had a lot of involvement with the youth diversion programmes, particularly since my retirement. I've always seen the juvenile courts as being able to play a crucial role in crime prevention, if those cases and offenders are approached in the right way. Judge John O'Connor at Smithfield was a visionary judge who ran a tight and effective court that I admired hugely. He also believed in getting the story behind the crime and in working with juveniles to try to get them on to another path. He did wonders simply by having a keen interest in people and a genuine desire to help them. I had long wanted to meet him, and one day he invited me to lunch at his home. I went to lunch... and left at 6 p.m. We just clicked and got on brilliantly with each other and talked for hours. I was very grateful to John for dedicating a bench book to me. A bench book sets out how cases are dealt with in a particular court – in this instance, the juvenile court. I was surprised at that because of my limited involvement in the juvenile courts, but the dedication noted my commitment to listening to defendants, which was equally important with juvenile criminals. I was really touched to get that nod of recognition.

When I was asked by then Garda Commissioner Nóirín O'Sullivan to chair a commission on reviewing the Garda Diversion Programmes, I was delighted to accept. I felt it was a chance to use my knowledge and my long-standing support for the diversion approach, and hopefully to make good inroads into improving the service. The Hussey Report was published in 2018, but I could not term it a success. I cited recommendations, but nothing has come to pass since then. Change tends to occur with glacial slowness in government departments, so this is not surprising. Although every once in a while a change can proceed with lightning swiftness, as happened with maternity leave for ministers in

2020. That happened very quickly, but other things, my report included, get put on the back burner for long periods. I would love to see the gardaí much more supported in what they are doing and trying to achieve, because it is most certainly for the good of everyone.

When a court becomes part of the wider justice community, it can aim higher and achieve more. I'd like to see every court become a living, hardworking part of its community. It is, after all, the people's justice system, there to serve us in our time of need. If it's a rarefied, solemn, convoluted place, it can't serve that purpose as well as it might. For my own part, my years on the bench confirmed in my mind that a court should and must be a hub, a point where all other points cross and meet, allowing for broader solutions to the problems brought before it. The court exists for the good of society, as part of society, and it's right that that should be its guiding force.

CHAPTER 8

BLAME IS CONVENIENT;
SECOND CHANCES OFTEN ARE NOT

t's often said that we live in a litigious society now, where people are quick to blame, quick to seek redress and quick to demand recompense. The criminal justice system is set up for this. In the higher courts, there is an adversarial approach, with defence and prosecution both trying to win – even if that might not equate to justice for most of us. The District Court is free to have a broader remit, if the judge so wishes. At Kilmainham, I tried to make my court a place where blame could be placed and acknowledged, but also where a second chance could be afforded wherever possible. It wasn't simply a blame game – it was justice with the aim of everyone being a winner. The very best iteration of that, from my point of view, was when the victim was satisfied and the accused got the opportunity to change their ways and not become yet another member of our expensive prison population.

I know this isn't a universal view. For some, once a person has been brought before a court of law, that means they are already 'less than' and deserving of punishment. After 84 years of observing human beings, my own view is that every one of us is capable of being a victim and equally capable of being a wrongdoer. No one has a special exemption from bad behaviour. Commonly, it's more a matter of circumstance than nature. I think there are very few evil people, just as there are probably very few truly good people. I don't think any of us can claim the luxury of being different or better.

It's hard to tell if evil is born or made. Perhaps a person is born with that possibility within them, and it could be worked out of them given certain favourable conditions – if they were born into a good, loving home, for example; conversely, that seed could easily progress in bad conditions. In court, I witnessed the legacy of circumstances again and again. I was the product of my upbringing, and that start in life made it easy for me to keep going on the straight and narrow. But if your upbringing is challenging, inadequate or downright diabolical, well, it's no wonder you end up doing the sorts of things that land you in court. That's not an excuse, but I do think it behoves us as a society to strive to understand the causes of crime, so that we can tackle them more efficiently and fairly.

I think that, in all my years on the bench, there was only one person who stood before me when still very young and yet already appeared to be beyond help. That was Warren Dumbrell, a young offender who was bred into badness and exhibited no desire to change. It was disturbing to meet a mere child and to realise that a combination of background, upbringing and attitude had forged a personality that cared not a jot for other people, or for redemption.

I first remember him as a young boy, aged about 12. A garda apprehended him and brought

him to Kevin Street Station. That was not techni-
cally the correct station (the correct station would
have put him outside of my bailiwick), but it was
the closest one and he was a young fella, so the
garda escorted him there. He then brought him to
Kilmainham and asked me to speak to him in my
chamber. The boy came into the chamber, accompanied by his mother and solicitor. We talked, and
I suggested we invite the Probation Service to get
involved. The boy's mother emphatically refused
this suggestion. That was the first and last time I
heard such a refusal.

In August 1986, the country was reeling in
the aftermath of Hurricane Charley, which had
torn a path across Ireland, taking the roof of my
house with it. I was out of my house for about
three months while I tried to put hearth and home
back together. My house was a hive of builders.
One day, a man stopped outside and asked if he
could take a look inside the house. One of the
builders recognised him as Warren Dumbrell's
father, a well-known criminal, and told him he
couldn't enter the property. Not long after that, I
was in court one morning when three men were

brought before me. I looked at them and thought, *Oh dear.* One was Mr Dumbrell and one was the brother of my builder – and, I think, the reason the builder was so well versed in notorious criminals. It was a minor offence that they were charged with, but because of that connection – and the fact that he had tried to gain access to my house – I immediately transferred them to be heard in the Bridewell.

From the time he was 12, Warren Dumbrell's potential for serious crimes was apparent. No interventions encouraged him to change. In 2006, he and his brother murdered Christopher Cawley in front of his wife and children. He has been in prison for years now. I still remember vividly his mother protesting against the involvement of the Probation Service. I think the family could simply see no other way of life. When you get a person like that, in a situation like that, it deprives them of the ability to be saved. It's a terrible thing to witness.

But that wasn't common, thankfully. The people in the dock were, in the majority, those who had fallen off the edges of society. They had never known any different. That was why the services that tried to broaden their horizons beyond a criminal way of life were so crucial. These people had to be shown different in order to understand it was there – and that it could be theirs.

Whenever I heard narrow-minded people waxing lyrical about ne'er-do-wells and the point-lessness of trying to help, I always thought of all the crimes committed on the 'right side' of the law. It is often the case that wrongdoing gets called by different names depending on who's involved, or their postcode: the junkie versus the recreational drug user; the lowlife versus the 'white collar, no one got harmed, deserves a different set of standards' criminal. It amazes me how people can describe their own actions to themselves to cover over the truth. I was struck, for example, by a recent rape case in county Kerry, where some local people gave character references for the man convicted of the crime. How awful for the young victim, I thought. I wouldn't be asking for references if I had done something wrong. Twice in my career I was asked for character references – once for a barrister and once for a garda. I refused both. To the best of my knowledge at the time, they were both guilty of wrongdoing, so on that basis I simply said, 'I'm sorry. I can't.'

An education and a good job do not mean a cast-iron character. I've seen offenders from every walk of life in the dock, from priests to middle-class professionals, to prison officers. There was that man in Dalkey, a widely respected pillar of society who stood accused of murder, and people like swimming coach Derry O'Rourke, who had comfortable, privileged lives but were also paedophiles. The dock was open to all types of people, from all strata in society. I myself have never committed a crime, but I have been the victim of crime. So when I say that I believe firmly in second chances, that's not coming from some idealised view of the world and those who live in it. It comes from an inside understanding of what it's like to be victimised, to be scared and to be angry. I've experienced that first-hand, but I would still argue for a justice system that uses every service at its disposal to try to intervene and pull criminals away from their bad choices to better ones. And I say this in full knowledge that second chances are always a gamble, because there's nothing sure about people.

I've been on the receiving end of criminal behaviour a number of times in my life. One Sunday morning, I was on Amiens Street, and I remember feeling uneasy. Looking back, it was like a sort of premonition. I was walking with my daughter, who was on her way to the train station with her young son and daughter, and the street was empty but for the four of us. The next thing, a fella shot past on a bike, snatching my handbag off my shoulder as he went. I have to admit, I was impressed by his speed and agility. If he'd chosen a different life, he could have been an Olympic athlete. I reported the theft to my local garda station, and they contacted Store Street. The garda who dealt with it there, a man I'd known for years, told me that they had found the young thief. He had admitted taking my bag, but he also said that he'd burned it after rifling through it and figuring out my identity.

I have been burgled twice – once when I lived in Ballsbridge, and once in my current home. Both times I was out, so I was spared any confrontation. The Ballsbridge robbery was, I'm quite sure, carried out by a man I gave a prison sentence to in Dún Laoghaire, when I was on the bench there.

His MO was distinctive, and he admitted to other burglaries that were similar to mine, although he never put up his hand about my house. But I knew. And the second time it happened, which was about 17 years ago, I was utterly furious with myself. I had bought a safe deposit box and put money and documents inside – and then I left it sitting on my bedroom floor. I mean, you'd really think I'd know better. I do know better! But I made a silly mistake, and there it was for the burglar – I may as well have wrapped it up with a bow. He just picked it up and waltzed out with it. How could I have been so daft? When the gardaí were called, a sergeant and a young uniformed garda turned up. I knew the sergeant. The next thing, a car pulled up and out stepped the chief super. I still laugh to think of the shock on the young garda's face when he saw the big boss taking on a local house break-in. I told the young garda before he left that I knew the chief super when he was the same age as him.

I've many friends who've also experienced burglaries, and they often describe an eerie feeling in the house afterwards and don't like being alone there. It never bothered me. It happened, it was over, and there I left it. I didn't dwell on it. However, I am very conscious of my personal safety, which is a legacy of my work as much as of those crimes. I'm very careful and alert when out walking alone and always conscious about my personal belongings. And now I have two fierce dogs that bark up a storm if anyone so much as looks at the house.

In terms of work-related crime experiences, the most intimidating were probably those carried out by the Cahill family. Martin Cahill, the notorious Ordinary Decent Criminal, had lots of young relatives, and they were a constant thorn in my side – although I suppose they'd say the same of me. I saw many of them in my court, mainly for burglaries. There was a street party one night in one of the flat complexes in Dublin 8 where several of the Cahills lived, and the gardaí were called out to it. They wanted to gain access to a particular house, but they didn't have a warrant. Eventually, however, they did get into the house in order to resolve the situation. Questions were raised over the legality of their entrance into the house. I sent a case stated to the High Court and received back a ruling that it was permissible for the gardaí to have entered the house in those circumstances. On that basis, I gave three or four of Cahill's gang an 18-month sentence. Not something that was going to endear me to the family.

One morning, when I lived in Ballsbridge, I looked out my window, and there were two gardaí on their bellies, looking under the cars. On the street outside my home, all of the car tyres had been neatly slashed – every single vehicle. Obviously, the Cahill clan didn't know that my car wasn't parked on the street. I had a side passage to my end-of-terrace house, and every evening when I got home, I would drive down the passage and into the adjacent garage to park. That was a very handy home arrangement for a judge on the criminal side of the bench, and I gave thanks for it that morning as I went to retrieve my perfectly intact car. My mostly elderly neighbours were very supportive, even though that must have been a frustrating incident for them. It was designed to intimidate me, but thankfully it only happened once.

The worst and most distressing crime of which I've been a victim was an attempted carjacking about four years ago, when I was 80 years old. It was St Patrick's weekend, and I was going to get my hair done. The salon was in a rather lonely spot in Citywest, surrounded by residential apartments. I parked outside, just behind another car that drove off and left me a lovely, easy parking space. I turned off the engine and gathered my things. The passenger door opened. A man I had never seen before leaned into the car and said, 'Can I have your car, please?' As he moved towards me, he repeated that same question three times. I finally gathered my wits and said, 'No', but my voice sounded so odd, like a little dog barking. I didn't sound like me at all. Mercifully, my hairdresser, Noeleen, had noticed my arrival and this exchange. She came running out, then ran back in and called the guards.

By the time the guards arrived, my hair was done. We had used the time well. I didn't know the two gardaí who responded to the call, but then a detective pulled up, and I did recognise him. I relayed my story and told them that the man who had tried to take my car was dressed in camouflage, so he was quite conspicuous. The detective asked me to go with him in his car and tasked one of the young gardaí to drive my car to Rathcoole Garda Station, where my statement would be taken. We headed off in convoy, but just at the exit from the motorway, the patrol car pulled up and told us that a man in camouflage had been spotted. We hared off in pursuit.

I spotted him walking along a street, alone. The detective's car, in which I was sitting, and the patrol car parked up just beyond him. The detective told me to stay put, and then he leapt out and went to arrest him. I couldn't see what was happening because it was taking place behind me, but I could hear loud screaming and yelling as the man determinedly resisted arrest. I was terrified. In the end, it took pepper spray and a backup patrol car to finally subdue him and get him safely into the back of the garda car. When the detective came back, his glasses were broken and he looked completely shook. I felt so sorry for him. But on we went to Rathcoole, where I gave my statement. The detective asked me how I was feeling, and I told him that I had been feeling okay, but now I felt stressed and shaky. It was a truly horrible experience to be the victim in that scenario. You never know how you're going to respond to violence or assault until it happens to you. But that sense of it about to happen makes you melt inside. That's what happened to me – my insides liquefied, and I felt sick with anticipation. It was a very disturbing experience.

The detective offered me a lift home, and I was glad to accept because I don't think I could have driven myself at that point. He deputed a young female garda to drive me, followed by a male garda driving my car. That night, while in a restaurant with friends, I got a call to say my would-be carjacker had been kept at the station all day and was now about to be released. The doctor had come to assess him, and it turned out he was a paranoid schizophrenic, a former social worker, from a good and supportive family, but he hadn't taken his meds recently. I said that I didn't want him prosecuted since that wouldn't solve his problem. I wanted him to seek the correct help, not be punished for it.

The following Monday, my doorbell rang. It was a dark night and I was still feeling nervous, so I opened a downstairs window and looked out. There on the step was a reporter who wanted to talk to me about the incident. I said, 'No way, it's sub judice,' and slammed the window shut. The truth was, the reporter had frightened me, and I was furious with him for that. I didn't dwell on that either, but it was striking how the effects of that attempted carjacking stayed with me. A few days later I was out strolling when a man came towards me, and something of his physique and walk reminded me of camouflage man. I absolutely froze. That experience really taught me how it feels to be a victim and how that can stay with you for so long. It's a very lonely feeling because no one else can fully understand since they weren't there and didn't experience it. It made me glad I had been accommodating towards victims in my time on the bench, given that this was how they were probably feeling.

There was another nasty experience, although it wasn't a crime against me as such – it was closer to the kind of public shaming so common online nowadays, although this was in the days before social media. It involved a case of mistaken identity, stemming yet again from a mix-up of the Hussey name, and it was another interesting insight into being on the wrong side of the bench.

One Wednesday morning, before court commenced, my registrar said to me, 'Did you hear your son was arrested last Saturday?' Apparently a garda had tipped him off that my son, Ronan, had been apprehended. I thought it was very funny and laughed it off. It didn't bother me in the slightest because I knew that my son had been out of the country on Saturday – plus he'd never been in trouble with the gardaí in his life, so to my ears it sounded preposterous.

That evening, I was speaking to Ronan, who was a photographer with the *Irish Independent*, and I told him about this funny remark. He, however, did not find it amusing in the slightest. He was furious that such a thing was being whispered about him. But it turned out to be a fortunate forewarning, because that Friday, Ronan went into work and his boss asked how he had got on in court that morning. Ronan replied that he hadn't been working that morning. His boss insisted he had been in court, as a defendant. Immediately, Ronan knew that my registrar's rumour had spread further afield.

That Saturday, I was talking on the phone with Ronan's boss, who wished to discuss a personal matter with me, and when I hung up, my phone immediately began ringing again. It was a reporter asking about my son's arrest. I was astonished by this, but he told me I ought to take a look at the *Irish Press* newspaper. I rang Ronan's boss again and asked him what was in the *Press*. He replied, 'Are you sitting down?' I sat down, and he read out the headline: 'Son of Beak done for Drunk and Disorderly'. The article stated that my son – I was 'the beak', an old nickname for a judge – had been arrested for dancing on the bonnet of a car in Dublin city centre, that he had been charged with drunk and disorderly, and that he had given a false name to the gardaí. Well!

I knew it couldn't have been Ronan because the offence had happened on a Saturday night, and Ronan had travelled to Scotland on the Friday in order to attend a rugby match on Saturday afternoon. I was rostered to court that night. I felt all sorts of emotions and wondered if I should cancel work and stay home, then decided it was best to face it now rather than later. As it was, no one mentioned it to me that night, but a few days later someone in court asked about my son being arrested. People were also asking Ronan about his outing to court, and he was not best pleased to have this false story circulating about him. The truth of the matter was that it was one of Ronan's cousins who had been arrested. The *Irish Press* reporter had seen the name 'Hussey' and jumped to the conclusion that it must be my son – even though the first name wasn't Ronan. It was an assumption that hadn't been fact-checked.

I went to my solicitor, who said this incident had to be taken seriously because it was a slur on the Hussey name. So Ronan and I both sued the *Irish Press*. They took us to the door of the Circuit Court, where they offered a settlement. It was settled, but I didn't live it down for the rest of my career. Criminals would shout at the gardaí, 'Forget about me, go arrest the judge's son.' It had a long-lasting effect that was very unpleasant. It was horrible to have people talking about my family, alleging things that were incorrect, sniggering, relishing the idea of me being taken down a peg or two. It was hard to keep facing that every day.

That's what I mean when I say that my view on second chances comes from a place of eyes-wide-open realism. I know full well what it feels like to be a victim and why the need for a trial is so pressing, because it can deliver closure to some extent. I know that, but I also know full well that people can change and that lives can be transformed, and I believe it's worth trying to achieve that. The victim must be supported and must receive justice, but there is more than one way to deliver justice. It's not one-size-fits-all. This is the whole point of a judge – to oversee the details of the individual case and weigh up the case on its own merits before reaching a judgment on the matter. And when a crime is fuelled by addiction, it's essential to investigate alternatives, because there's a person hidden beneath the addiction, and if you can excavate them back out into the light, you might find they are very different from the person you met in court.

When I look back over my court days, I met people in the dock who later became well-adjusted, contributing members of society. I find that wonderful. They are thriving and on a completely new path, having put the old ways far behind them. What is also often the case is that they are engaged in work to help others who are still lost in the old ways. That has always struck me: if you got one person out, they went on to get others out. It was a positive chain reaction. What I learned over time was that it could be very fortunate for a person to appear in court. If you had a good judge and a good court that was alive to the possibilities for justice, a negative act and experience could turn into a positive opportunity for change. I always hoped that victims understood that that was what I was trying to do – to make life better for the victim and for the accused, for everyone's benefit.

Of course, a second chance doesn't automatically mean leniency. Sometimes the only way to deliver a second chance was through a custodial sentence, which could serve as a rude awakening. I remember a night when I received a call from John Lonergan. I had put a young woman and her child in custody for a week for handbag snatching. (This was before the Dóchas centre opened.) Poor John asked if he could send her down to me at Kilmainham the following day. I said, 'No. Why?' And he replied, 'I have to go out and buy nappies tonight.' It was a half-joking comment, but it was the case that a baby or child in the prison was extremely difficult for the staff and the prison operations. They wished to avoid it, if at all possible – for everyone's sake. Much as I felt sorry for John, I knew that girl needed a taste of custody. I could have organised for her to return to court and be released on bail given that she had no prior convictions, but I wasn't minded to do that. She had turned up in my court with her child in tow in a bid to influence my decision, but I saw putting the child through that as a malicious act. *Forget it*, I thought. I was not going to be hamstrung by that performance. I put her and the child into custody. But the end of that story was that I never saw that young woman again. She had learned a hard lesson.

My belief in second chances led to my involvement with various addiction services and centres. I was always delighted to be asked to serve on a board or as a patron, and I still undertake that work to this day. I was involved for many years in Coolmine and then Shechem House, and I am patron of the St James's Camino Residential Centre for men and Tiglin residential centres for men and women. All of these centres work with people involved in addiction, giving them the 24/7 support and care they need in order to break the habit and leave drugs behind. As a judge, I had the easy job of being aware of this option and nudging people towards the Probation Service, where they might be recommended to avail themselves of it. However, the people working in these centres have the terrifically difficult job of helping folks take responsibility for their addictions and their recovery. That requires enormous dedication and commitment, and the patience of a squadron of saints. But they do it with grace, humour and respect, and I am privileged to be able to witness that – and its effects – up close.

St James's Camino was set up by Fr Denis Laverty, who was also on the board of WHAD. He has spent his entire adult life tending to those with alcohol- and drug-addiction problems. He is so humble and hesitant to accept praise, but I know he deserves it. He encourages the residents to do lots of walking, to walk back to themselves as it were, walk out their troubles. He calls it 'the long walk of addiction'. Many of them also undertake the Camino walk in Spain, Portugal and France, which can be transformative. I'm a patron of the residential centres, where residents stay for

13–14 weeks, on average, before graduating. I've been attending the graduations for years, and I've seen the average age of the residents rise from the mid-to-late thirties to anything up to the sixties. The age profile of addiction has expanded, as have the substances – where once heroin was common, now there is so much addiction to prescription drugs, painkillers and sleeping pills. I remember chatting to a well-dressed man at a recent graduation ceremony. He caught my eye because he looked out of place, so I went over to find out his story. He told me that he had suffered a back injury and become addicted to the painkillers prescription to help him. He had gone to the Camino centre to wean himself off them – and he had successfully kicked the habit. He told me he had done it for his family. This is an interesting development in drug addiction, and it means the services are required even more now, and by many more people.

When I speak at the Camino graduations, I always take care to address the families of the residents directly. They can be a bit forgotten in the midst of the addiction and treatment, but their care and support are crucial. They, too, have to dig in for the long haul and devote themselves to their loved one's well-being, and I admire them greatly for doing so. I often say to the family members that it's a long walk for them, too, that they suffer as well, and so it's important to have the graduation as a celebration for everyone going the distance.

I have been involved with many people and places dealing with addiction, but I have to say that Tiglin is so important in the story of my life and work. I've already described the inimitable Aubrey McCarthy, who founded it and keeps it going with energy and good humour, ably partnered by his friend and CEO Phil Thompson. The origin story of Tiglin is extraordinary, and I'm so proud to have played a small part in it.

In the early 1990s, I received a letter from Alan and Barbara Sweetman, the managers of Shechem House, a women's aid centre. The letter described the life and progress of a young girl, and it intrigued me. I rang Alan, and he invited me to visit the centre and see the work they were doing there. I went down and was introduced to 10 young women who were all staying in a lovely bungalow, being helped and cared for by the Sweetmans. I was very taken by it: it seemed very well run, and I could tell they knew what they were at.

After that first visit, I stayed in touch and attended Shechem House's summer party every year. Following my retirement, I went to a sale of work they were holding. There, Alan told me there was someone who wanted to see me. He brought me over to meet a young woman, who told me that I had once put her in custody for a week. Her name was Gillian, too, and I remembered her because her mother had wept in the court, pleading for her daughter to receive help. Those tears were deeply felt and deeply affecting. Gillian had been on bail and was rearrested, and she appeared in the custody of a garda. Her mother beseeched me to 'do something with her'. I decided to tell the mother that she would know where her daughter was for the next seven days and nights, and I put Gillian in custody again. A week later, I released her on bail. As I did so, I told this waif in the dock that she could change her life or I might have to interfere again. I put the case back for two months, requesting that a probation report be prepared. I didn't tell her I was retiring in three weeks' time. Young Gillian subsequently got clean and turned her life around. That day at the sale of work, we chatted like old friends. I ended up attending her graduation and, later, her wedding. She now has four sons, and we are still friends.

The two Gillians were asked to give a speech at a fundraising dinner, to tell our story from sentencing to friendship. We agreed, and it went very well. During that speech, I made a throwaway remark. I was describing Shechem House and what it had meant to Gillian, and I said something like, 'Such a pity there is no centre like this for men.' Little did I know that Aubrey McCarthy was in the audience that night, and he picked up my throwaway remark and ran with it, as only Aubrey can. The end result was that he set up Tiglin with his right-hand man, CEO Phil Thompson, who is responsible for Tiglin running as smoothly as it does on a day-to-day basis. They established a men's residential centre at Ashford in County Wicklow. I made another speech at the Glenview Hotel in Wicklow one night, and that resulted in the donation of a building in Brittas Bay, which became a women's centre for Tiglin. There is also a centre in Naas that provides homelessness services, and a homeless drop-in centre on Pearse

Street in Dublin called The Light House. Tiglin has now helped hundreds of men – and women – to come back from addiction and crime and to restart their lives. It is utterly astonishing to me that all this has flowed from a casual remark. But then, I was so fortunate to meet a person of the calibre of Aubrey McCarthy.

The most recent addition to the growing list of Tiglin centres is Carraig Eden in Greystones. It's a huge, beautiful centre, and I attended the opening in 2021. I met President Michael D. Higgins there and his wife Sabina, and it was a magnificent day. One man came over to me and asked if I understood the legacy I was leaving to the nation, and I nearly cried at that. He meant that Tiglin arose from our speech that night, and I was so touched that people would link me with this marvellous achievement. The launch of Carraig Eden was a joint project between Tiglin and Wicklow County Council, with the council buying the building and donating it to Tiglin. President Higgins noted in his speech that it would be wonderful if other county councils followed suit, and he was perfectly correct. And there is, in fact, another such collaboration under way in Kildare, at Jigginstown Manor, which Tiglin has taken over, so the message is getting through.

A place like Tiglin is so badly needed, and only good flows from it. It's those who have been helped going on to help others, and that's a wonderful thing to see. It absolutely warms my heart. Tiglin has now linked with the Institute of Technology Carlow to give the residents the option of studying IT or other subjects to graduate level. That gives them a head start when re-entering the world after addiction, because that can be a tricky transition. But they emerge from Tiglin ready for employment.

I visit Tiglin often and always get so much from chatting to the residents and staff. I was in the men's centre one day, and a chap came up to me and said that I'd given him his first sentence, years before. 'What in hell took you so long to get here?' I asked him. One of the managers of Carraig Eden is an old friend of mine, a formidable woman called Jessica. Not only had she appeared in my dock as a young woman, but she was one of the women I had first met at Shechem House. I remembered her well, because she had pleaded for her case not to be sent forward to the Circuit Court, but I did send it forward because I felt she was on a very slippery slope and headed in only one direction. She likes to tell me that I was harsh on her – and I was, deliberately so – but she is glad of it because she changed her life after that experience. She is devoted to helping others now and offering them the same chances she was given and took. At the opening of Carraig Eden, Jessica took a treasured photograph of me meeting President Higgins, then she added a crown above my head and sent it to me with the caption, *Our queen*. That made me laugh. She recently appeared on television, on RTÉ, and was most impressive.

One of the most remarkable stories from Tiglin is that of Derek 'Deky' Byrne. He never came before me in Kilmainham, since he wasn't living in my jurisdiction, but he was a very familiar face to the Courts Service. He was a chronic drug addict, came from an incredibly tough family background and had committed many crimes. I'm quite sure anyone who met him in those years would have been convinced he'd soon end up dead, one way or another. But against all the odds, Deky signed in to

Tiglin, where he had an inspiring counsellor who did wonders for him. Deky turned his life around, got out of the drug scene and then started helping others to escape. He has now set up a company called Way2Work, in conjunction with Tusla Child and Family Agency, and with the support and backing of two West of Ireland businessmen, John Killeen and John Osborne. Way2Work provides training and work experience to young men, to bring them back into society after their lives have been somewhat derailed. The construction company Sisk & Co. is very involved as well. There's a nice sense of full circle to that, since my uncle Anthony – to whom I was apprenticed – acted for John Sisk Senior, so I knew Mr Sisk in my youth and he was a lovely gentleman. Way2Work has been hugely successful, and I've watched on in admiration as Deky, now an old friend, has forged this new path for himself.

All of these stories revolve around a second chance being given – and accepted. That's the key, of course. The court, via the Probation Service, can offer the opportunity, but after that it's entirely up to the person to take it and make something of it. If they're not ready to do that, it will fall on deaf ears and come to nothing. But if it happens when the time is right, it really is amazing what a difference it can make. I've seen so many lives that looked like miserable cul-de-sacs and then, with just that little nudge, the horizon opens up suddenly and there's a whole new vista to move towards. It's very, very possible, even when things look hopeless, which is why second chances – and addiction centres – have a crucial place in any decent society or courtroom.

CHAPTER 9

SILENCE IS A RIP CURRENT THAT DRAGS EVERYONE UNDER

There is a lot of talk now about how much Ireland has changed in the past 20 years. It has certainly been a time of rapid change – not just the rise of the digital era, but also the new legislation that has paved the way for same-sex marriage, divorce, abortion and greater scope in tackling domestic abuse, thanks to the subsection on coercive control inserted into the Domestic Violence Act 2018. These are all fantastic steps in progressing us as a society, and I applaud them – indeed, I voted for them at the ballot box. I think there's a common view of elderly people as constantly harking back to the past, nostalgic for 'the good old days', but I don't subscribe to that way of thinking at all. I can plainly see the changes that have taken place over the course of my lifetime, the contrast between then and now, and I'm very happy to live in the now and to keep learning and moving with the times. That approach is what keeps a person young, engaged and sharp, which is how I want to be as I age.

The courtroom is, of course, a microcosm of society, and from the bench you can see the issues and challenges that the country has to tackle. Whenever we faced recession, for example, it manifested in the courtroom in a spate of drugs, burglary, domestic abuse and fraud charges. Everything that happens at the macro level trickles down one way or another into people's daily lives. I've watched with great interest as those issues have changed over the years. I realise now that there were great silences blanketing people's lives in the first three-quarters of the 20th century, and that those silences hid great and devastating wrongdoing. It's worth keeping those lessons in mind as we continue to progress and try to create a safer and fairer society for everyone.

Going back to my early days, both in life and on the bench, religion played a huge role in creating and maintaining those silences. It really has an awful lot to answer for. The other huge problem with the religious hierarchy was that it instituted a one-way system of absolute and unearned respect. Men of the cloth expected to be treated with deference, and they were. The whole country colluded in raising up these men to an 'untouchable' level and, in doing so, ensured they could act with impunity behind closed doors. I've seen this attitude again in my lifetime with some in the judiciary and in politics who saw themselves as above other people, and therefore above the law. Whenever respect is abused in this manner, it always ends badly. When I look back now, the power of the Church was dreadful. The idea of John Charles McQuaid giving dispensations to Catholics to study at 'Protestant' Trinity College Dublin is just appalling. I love to mention that to young people and watch their faces as they move from laughter to horror at the idea of it. I was watching a *Prime Time Investigates* programme recently about the birth certificates scandal related to the mother and baby homes, and up came a photo of Éamon de Valera, his son Éamon de Valera Jnr, who was a gynaecologist, and John Charles McQuaid, all together. I found myself thinking, *If they were alive today, they'd probably be in prison.*

The silences created by the Catholic Church and its teachings ranged from the daft to the dangerous. As an example of the plain daft, I remember walking with my mother and meeting a good friend of mine, who was also with her mother. I would have been about 19 years old at the time, my friend about 24. My friend was married, I had served as her chief bridesmaid at the wedding, and she was now happily pregnant, about six months along. We all chatted, but no one mentioned the fact that she was pregnant. It was the most bizarre conversation – talk about the elephant/pregnant woman in the room. Afterwards, I brought it up with my mother and was brusquely told that no one had wished to discuss such an indelicacy in front of someone as young as me, an unmarried maiden. That silence was ludicrous: my friend's pregnancy was as plain as the noses on our faces, yet we all made a show of pretending not to know or notice. Why on earth did we go along with that?

As a country, we also went along with the mother and baby homes, which will be forever to our discredit. I didn't know what was going on at the time it was happening, and the revelations of the past 10 years have left me feeling guilty and disgusted. But I did not have any idea that the religious orders were engaged in such immoral and illegal dealings, and I have to presume many others didn't know either, if they hadn't experienced it first-hand. It shocks me, but at the same time it doesn't fully surprise me, because so much was protected by those silences. When people are afraid to speak out, the silence becomes more and more powerful, until it feels like a complete impossibility to break it. That's what happened in Ireland in those dark times, I think. We lost the belief that we could resist, and that things didn't have to be that way.

For my own part, I did have professional dealings with one mother and baby home, but it never led to any suspicion that the women there were being abused in any way. My employer Denis

Greene, solicitor, acted for the women in the home on the Navan Road. Whenever the women came by on business matters, I was asked to vacate my office so they could use it for signing documents. I was a mere 21 years of age then, so my eyes were out on stalks to see these 'fallen women'. They never looked upset, distressed, beaten into compliance or anything like that. They were very normal women, not very young, often on their second, third and sometimes even fourth baby. They came to our office because we had a wealthy American client who adopted children from the Navan Road home. He was a devout Catholic, with an oratory in his house. He and his wife wished to adopt six children from Ireland, and our office organised the paperwork. So when the women came to use my office, they were signing adoption papers for this gentleman. In the end, he adopted five children from the home. But as I said, I saw no sign whatsoever of duress on the part of those women. I do hope that was the case.

Strangely enough, there is an unexpected postscript to this story. About three years ago, I was visiting the now-retired Detective Tom Madden – the one who had brought me out on that infamous drug squad night patrol. He told me a story about a case he had been involved in out in Dún Laoghaire, although it took place after my time on the bench there. The case involved a youngish man who lived in Dalkey and who was found in possession of a small amount of illegal drugs. After becoming fascinated by this man and his backstory, Tom would sit and have coffee with him and hear about his life. He told me that the young man was one of five children adopted from the Navan Road, that he had been sent to America to a wealthy couple and that he'd had a good life with them. Imagine Tom's surprise when I was able to fill in the rest of that story. It was an extraordinary coincidence, but I was glad to learn that those five babies had been well cared for.

That was my only direct experience with women who had gone through a mother and baby home. When I learned in recent years of the extent of the abuse often suffered by the girls sent to the homes, it was a nasty shock. It's uncomfortable to know that a blanket of silence could be used so effectively, smothering out any opposition, even any knowledge of what was going on. People must not have talked about it, even if they did know – or, at least, no one of my acquaintance ever did. I can only presume there was a deep silence on the matter, that the girls didn't speak openly for fear of what might happen to them, that their families kept totally quiet on the matter out of fear of humiliation, and that anyone who witnessed the abuse also kept quiet and didn't report it. Or else reported it, but the gardaí involved chose to maintain the silence. It is quite incredible what fear can make people do – or not do.

At the time, there was also a huge silence around sex and sexual offences. During my early years on the bench, we never heard cases involving sexual offences – they simply did not come before the court. More silence. People were scared at the prospect of reporting such offences and having to speak publicly of them in a courtroom – and, unfortunately, this is something that is very slow to change. While there has been much progress on training gardaí and judiciary to deal with sexual assault survivors and perpetrators, it is still the case that victims can be put through a terrible ordeal if the case goes to trial. I saw progress on this over my years on the bench, but not enough, quite frankly.

Women and victims can still get a raw deal in court, and it's not right. My hope is that there will continue to be progress and training, so that these cases are dealt with effectively and fairly for all concerned.

It was in the late 1980s that sexual offences first began to appear on the roster at Kilmainham. In hindsight, I feel sorry for those pioneers who brought those early cases, because none of us – gardaí and judiciary – had any training whatsoever in that regard. We simply did not talk about such things then. I remember a scout leader who had committed a sexual offence that the DPP had classed as 'minor' and therefore to be dealt with in the District Court. I know, looking back, that I didn't deal with it properly. I wasn't sufficiently clued in, and the whole response to the victim – from gardaí to court – would have been inadequate. It's hard to admit, but it is true nonetheless. We had no training and no real understanding of the matter, because it was being spoken of for the very first time in that setting.

That was the start of it, though, and we all had to learn on the job as more and more cases came through the court. I have already recounted the trial of Fr Tony Walsh. I'm proud that I made the right decision that day, against all the odds. I also had Fr Brendan Smyth, the serial child abuser, brought before me. That was a night court, for which Smyth was transported down to the Bridewell from a prison in Northern Ireland, where he was already serving a sentence. After he was brought in, he slumped down on to a bench and remained in that position throughout the proceedings. He never moved or spoke. He was an overweight, jowly man, very unpleasant in appearance and unforgettable once seen. I heard that the prison officers could hear him in the back of the van as they drove down, passing unsavoury comments any time he spied a young boy out through the small window in his prison transport. I disliked him on sight due to his slovenly appearance and his disrespectful slouching. He was very different from Tony Walsh, who was a clean-shaven, good-looking man who didn't fit any idea anyone might have had of a paedophile. Smyth was the opposite. The court was empty and quiet, but his brooding presence seemed to fill the room. It was claustrophobic. I remanded him in custody and was glad never to set eyes on him again.

From then on, the silent abuses hidden in Irish society started to float to the surface regularly. This was a good thing, because it meant victims were finding the courage to speak up. And it led to further good things, in that the judicial system had to put in place the support system for these victims. Organisations like Victim Support were established around this time to provide this crucial service to facilitate victim reporting and prosecution at trial. Those early victims who came forward and pressed charges were extraordinarily courageous. We owe them a huge debt of gratitude, because it was their actions that pushed these offences into the national consciousness and on to the court agenda.

In the 1990s, a scandal emerged from Irish swimming, with a number of male coaches accused of rape and sexual assault. The case of swimming coach Derry O'Rourke went through Kilmainham. I remember that day well because the court was very full but unusually quiet. The place was packed to the rafters, with lots of young girls and their parents there to see O'Rourke in the dock, as well as extra security provided by An Garda. And yet the court wasn't noisy, as it normally was. The proceedings were accompanied by a most un-District Court-like atmosphere of quiet attention. It was very strange. I noted that the accused was sitting with his wife and family, who were there to support him. There weren't going to be any witnesses or victims speaking from the dock, so it was a very straightforward hearing remanding him for a Book of Evidence to send him forward for trial in the higher courts. That's why it was so odd to have a large number of people in attendance to see it. But O'Rourke had harmed many people, and it was obviously important to them to see the start of justice being done.

By contrast, there was another child abuse case that I remember well. This involved a man called Kevin Kavanagh, who was accused of abusing his three daughters. He looked like a typical grandfather type, very innocuous. In his case, his family were also in court, but not to support him. I looked on with interest as he took his seat to my left and his family took theirs to my right. They would obviously have nothing to do with him. Again, he had been remanded for a Book of Evidence, and on a further remand I sent him forward for trial in the Circuit Court. While I was signing the relevant documents, his solicitor requested that his client sit at the back of the room as he was feeling unwell. I agreed that he could do so, but that he would have to return to his place for the sending forward. When I was ready, Kavanagh came back up and stepped into the dock. The next thing, he fainted. An ambulance was called, and he was brought to St James's Hospital. The reactions of the gardaí, in particular, caught my eye: they didn't look remotely sympathetic. It turned out this display of frailty was for my benefit, and the gardaí had seen it all before. Years later, Kavanagh's daughters wrote a memoir about their traumatic childhood experiences, and I noted that he did his sentence for abusing his daughters, then lived alone, died alone and was buried alone. His day in court was a foreshadowing of the rest of his life.

These types of cases became horribly common across the Courts Service, but there were still those that could shock on account of their violence and gruesomeness. The case of Michael Bambrick was one of those. He stood in Kilmainham accused of killing and dismembering two women, both of whom were his girlfriend at the time of their murders. I sent him forward for trial and was very glad to see the back of him. He had a strange aura about him and the weirdest eyes I've ever seen – they never focused properly and something about them was profoundly disturbing. We have seen far too many cases of women murdered by their partners since then.

Later on, there was an appetite to try to break some of these silences, give victims a proper voice and face what had been done as a society. After I retired in 2002, I was invited by the Catholic hierarchy to chair the Catholic Church Commission on Child Sexual Abuse. This commission was set up by the Bishops' Conference and the Conference of Religious in Ireland, and it pledged to provide an impartial, independent investigation into allegations of sexual abuse by clerics. It comprised a retired judge, a social worker, a barrister, a psychologist, a retired garda, a former senator, a childcare worker and a forensic scientist. It was a massive undertaking, because it encompassed all of the abuses alleged to have been carried out by members of the Church. This meant that a huge number of religious orders had to be put into the contract, which set out the parameters of the investigation, listing every single order and church involved. Nothing like this had ever been done before, not on this scale. We got under way in June 2002, but there were all sorts of complications – not least that victims felt the Church should not be permitted to investigate itself, as they saw it.

As the months wore on, I became more and more worried about our ability to complete this mammoth task and about the toll it might take on me personally, given the time and energy it was going to consume. But then, fate stepped in in the form of my old sparring partner, Michael McDowell, who was then Minister for Justice. He announced the establishment of a statutory inquiry, which would interview the same witnesses and largely have the same remit. I discussed my concerns about this with the other members of the committee, and they agreed with my view that we should disband. I then went to the Catholic hierarchy and told them that we weren't going to continue because to do so would be unfair on the victims, asking them to recall their testimony twice, for two separate inquiries. They too agreed.

The statutory inquiry was set up, headed by Circuit Court Judge Yvonne Murphy. I have to be honest and say that I was very relieved. It was an onerous task, and the state was in a better position to complete it. The *Report of the Commission of Investigation into the Catholic Archdiocese of Dublin* was finally published in 2009 and became known as the *Murphy Report*. It came hard on the heels of the Commission to Inquire into Child Abuse, or the *Ryan Report*, which was an investigation conducted by Judge Sean Ryan into abuses at industrial schools. The substance of those reports was grotesque and deeply shocking. It showed conclusively that silence allows people to do terrible things, providing the conditions in which evil can thrive.

I was very glad that the official silence had been broken with the publication of those reports. But I was haunted by a feeling that I had to break that silence for myself as well, on a personal level. I had been a practising Catholic up to that point. I wouldn't have classed myself as very devout, and my children had already chosen to leave the Church, but I did have a faith that was part of my life. But now, I was so disgusted by the revelations about the crimes of these priests, and the culture of secrecy that had facilitated and protected them,

that I felt I could no longer be part of the organi-
sation they professed to represent.

One Sunday evening, I sat down and typed a long
letter to the Archbishop of Dublin, Diarmuid Martin.
In it, I told him that as a result of several things,
I was taking my leave of the Church. These things
included the *Murphy Report*, the *Ryan Report*, the
case of Fr Tony Walsh and the fact that my former
husband had been granted a Church annulment of
our marriage in a jurisdiction where I'd never lived
and where I didn't believe he had ever lived either. I
set it all out, my disillusion and disgust, and I posted
the letter the following morning.

On Tuesday, I received an email from the
Courts Service: 'Please ring Monsignor So-and-so
at Bishop's House.' I didn't call the Monsignor.
Within 36 hours, I received a letter of invitation
to the Archbishop's Palace in Drumcondra. I
accepted that invitation. When I arrived at the
Palace, I was brought into a room and introduced
to Archbishop Martin. I spent several hours with
him that day, talking non-stop. I have nothing but
the highest regard for Diarmuid Martin. He didn't
try to persuade me to change my mind, instead he

listened and offered thoughtful responses. He was a man of integrity, and I respected that. I enjoyed our conversation, but it didn't change my thoughts or feelings on the matter. I left the Church and ceased all contact with religion and its rituals. I don't regret it. I may not be a paid-up member of an institution anymore, but I fully believe in living a good life and being there for whoever needs my help. I suppose I still lead a Christian life, but I refuse to be part of a hierarchy that allowed systemic child abuse for decades. I can't stay silent about that.

While silence still poses a danger to Irish society, I can see the progress that has been made, and I'm very glad of it. We have learned some lessons and we have applied that knowledge. I had reason to sit in a courtroom in recent years for the hearing of a sexual offence case. I was there as a visitor, supporting a friend, for a sentencing hearing. There were 14 victims of this particular perpetrator, and I was very impressed by the decision of Judge Melanie Greally. In reading her judgment, she quoted from all 14 victim impact statements, and clearly she had engaged deeply with the victims' accounts. Had I been one of those victims, I would have felt justice had been done that day. I was pleased to see how the case was handled, not only for those involved, but for everyone beyond the court door. It felt like a progressive, listening, empathetic court, which is the way it should be. The case was handled correctly and with a clear understanding of sexual assault and its effects on survivors. If we keep learning from our past mistakes, and if specific training is incorporated into judges' continuous professional development, our courts can become the non-adversarial spaces for justice that we would all like them to be.

There is a new element in terms of sexual offences now, and that is pornography. It isn't 'new', of course, but the constant and instant availability of it in the digital age is a relatively recent development. This is where our looking to the past and learning from it can be helpful. We know that we shouldn't allow this part of life to become enveloped in silence, because that will only give it more power. It is important that, as a society, we confront the problem, size it up accurately and talk about it as grown-ups. We don't want to repeat the mistakes of the past. I was struck by this recently, when a judge was handing down a sentence in the case of a teenage boy who had raped a young family member. The judge noted clearly that pornography was now being viewed by children as young as 10, and that society would have to tackle this problem head-on. She is dead right. This is a very serious issue. When children are exposed to such images, it can warp their view of women and of sexual relationships. This is not something we can shy away from as a society.

What struck me most was that I distinctly recalled listening to child psychologist David Coleman speaking on the radio some years before. He had said then that children as young as 10 years of age were accessing and viewing pornography, which was shocking to hear at the time. A woman rang in and outlined her problem: she wanted to tell her eight-year-old son about the facts of life. Her husband disagreed, arguing that the boy was too young. She wanted to know David Coleman's opinion on the matter. He told her that speaking about it openly was the correct approach in his view, and that if there was a silence, things like porn would rush in to fill the void. I thought he was perfectly correct and admired both his direct approach and the value he placed on education and information. So, while I agreed wholeheartedly with the trial judge in that recent case, I was also thinking that this had been raised years ago, though obviously not enough people heard it then. Once again, it was an issue that was enveloped in silence, which means many people are realising only now what some have been saying for years. We can be terribly slow on the uptake, unfortunately.

I remember when the first application was made for a warrant relating to pornography, which occurred during my time in Kilmainham. This was all brand new to me – I grew up in 1940s and '50s Ireland, where sex was barely acknowledged, even though women were having very large families. It was a truly preposterous silence. But it was shattered first by the sexual offences coming to court, and then by the child pornography charges. The Pornography Act 1998 provided the legislative framework for the gardaí to make arrests. The very first warrant I was asked to issue in relation to a house search was for a solicitor in Dublin 4. Warrants two and three were for senior bankers living in County Wicklow. The gardaí involved in the search told me how the wife of one of the bankers answered the door to them and when they explained their purpose and showed the warrant, she replied, 'But what's wrong? He's only looking. He doesn't do anything.' The gardaí were astounded. This man had been viewing child pornography. One of the gardaí said to the woman, 'But those are real children. That's real suffering.' She seemed to have stopped up her ears to the truth, so that she could live her nice life and not be forced to confront what her husband was doing. I was astounded when the gardaí described this exchange to me. It just shows how people can accept the silence and choose to live inside it.

Domestic abuse is another huge area of concern in this regard. It is a massive problem in this country, but there is that same blanket of silence around so much of it. On the bench, I noticed with interest that working-class people were far quicker to report domestic violence and seek help. By contrast, it was middle-class people who tended to live with it for years and never utter a word to anyone. I felt it stemmed from a sense of shame in front of the neighbours about having the gardaí land on the doorstep. A woman who made that call, who went public about what was happening behind her closed door, was tearing down the pretty facade that made her life look normal and perfect to others. It can take great courage to do that.

But it is important to remember that there might be children behind those closed doors. In the case of wealthy families, those children are likely attending private school and have all the material comforts, so people are perhaps not interested in listening to their problems. Who do they tell? It's a kind of irony that working-class children who get involved in the justice system can then access help through the Probation Service or community organisations. When they stray off the path, there are people there trying to bring them back. But that isn't so much the case for the children of well-off families. They can face the difficulty of being expected to have no troubles and never complain because they 'have so much'. These children, by contrast, have very few supports. It's a funny thing that while money can buy you luxuries, it also often buys you isolation and a distinct lack of sympathy – regardless of age. From where I was sitting, those from less privileged backgrounds had a much greater chance of dealing with the issue of domestic violence than their counterparts in well-off areas.

Denial is a destructive form of silence, and I saw it constantly. I remember a young man whose girlfriend got on to me to ask for help. He was an accountant, and their life looked good from the outside, but he was struggling with alcohol addiction. His parents were alcoholics, and they had passed the baton to him. I couldn't help them, though I felt so sorry for his girlfriend. He could not see that he needed help, therefore he couldn't accept help. He hadn't reached the point where he could acknowledge the truth about himself. I saw that same problem with drug addicts. I was ready to engage the Probation Service and secure the offer of a second chance, but if they weren't ready to take it, there was no way it was going to help. If they were in denial, they were beyond help. It took time for me to admit and accept that, but it really was the truth of the matter that no one could force them into changing.

That said, I think there are encouraging signs now of a new willingness to speak up and seek help. When I went on the criminal side first, I remember thinking, *I wish the pendulum would swing towards more freedom, less silence.* But then I was exposed to all this crime, and I realised that the pendulum had swung too far, towards too much freedom. For example, in 2021 I was deeply shocked to see women at an anti-vaccine protest in Dublin who were launching themselves at the gardaí, kicking and punching. It was disgraceful behaviour. I was looking at those women and thinking that I wouldn't like to have to live with them. And it made sense to me, then, that the number of calls to Men's Aid keeps rising. I have read that they are reporting 25–30 calls a day from distressed men. I'm very glad those men have the guts to seek out the support that is there for them, but I'm also very sad that it has come to this. I had hoped the pendulum would swing towards decent equality, but it often looks like people want the right to be equally bad instead.

So here I am, wishing the pendulum would swing back somewhat again – and I promised not to give in to nostalgia and hark back to the way it was. It's a tightrope walk, balancing out the needs of society and the needs of the individual. I wouldn't want to swing back to my childhood because that horrible silence was covering so much and causing such devastation in people's lives. We can't go back there. But where we are now doesn't seem to be working for many people, either. That means we have to go forward and find a new level. We are still charting a course through our new world of technology, and it's going to take time to figure it all out. Smartphones and other devices are wonderful – and I'm an avid user of them – but surveillance culture breeds distrust, and humans don't do well when they are unsure what or who to trust. We've seen that played out across the world recently, right into the halls of the Capitol in Washington. It's an interesting time to be alive, I'll say that.

There is always hope, though. It's important to remember that the good in the world is often silent, too. There are so many people quietly beavering away, making the world around them a better place. On days when the court was stuffed to the gills with those who had caused chaos, it was always helpful to remember the silent good-doers who worked diligently and sought no recognition. I've

LESSONS FROM THE BENCH

met plenty of those people, too, thankfully. There are two in particular that embody this notion: two brothers I met through Aubrey McCarthy of Tiglin.

Aubrey came across two young boys living in the Phoenix Park, where they were eking out a dangerous existence on the very edge of society. They were from Croatia and had escaped a terrible life there, ending up in Ireland. They spoke no English. They were traumatised. They were homeless. But they had one bit of good fortune: Aubrey spotted them. He put them in an Airbnb and helped them to adjust and integrate. When I first met them, not only did they speak no English, they didn't speak at all. They kept their eyes cast down to the floor and said nothing. However, with Aubrey's help, they began to recover, they learned English and they helped out in Tiglin.

Jay and Allen Bobinac are now in their twenties and heavily involved in helping others via Tiglin. When Jay was running a homeless help centre in Jigginstown, he contacted me and invited me out for lunch, to see the centre and its work. I was so pleased that the silent boy I had met was proposing lunch together, and I was thrilled to see the transformation that had taken place in this young man. We chatted over lunch, he showed me around, and I looked on in delight as he pointed out all the ways they help those less fortunate. He and his brother are the silent helpers (but now with a voice), devoted to making other people's lives better, which is remarkable after all they've been through, and in an adopted country, too. Jay has moved to Tiglin at Carraig Eden in Greystones for the moment. Both he and his brother Allen have got excellent qualifications from the Institute in Carlow, and I can only say they are so impressive and such an asset to Tiglin. It is essential to remember and acknowledge that there is quiet goodness at work in the world, and we are all the better for it.

CHAPTER 10

TO SERVE JUSTICE,
WE NEED A LEVEL PLAYING FIELD AND
ORDINARY, DECENT JUDGES

I t always amuses me when people hold assumptions based on my age, gender or former occupation. I was out to lunch with a friend recently, and when the waiter asked, 'Would you like the bill?' I said, 'No. I'd rather not have to pay the bill.' He looked startled, but when I began to laugh, he burst out laughing too, and we had a great chat. I don't think he was expecting a 'little old lady' to be smart with him. I've always enjoyed playing with those assumptions, especially when people think a judge is some sort of elevated, special person with divinely inspired wisdom. I've no time for that thinking. Judges are normal people doing a job. They are no better and no worse than anyone else in the courtroom. As far as I'm concerned, the best way to serve justice is to ensure that everyone receives equal respect and that everyone can do their job to the best of their ability – in other words, a level playing field presided over by an ordinary, decent judge.

One of the main barriers to a court based on equality is where the legal people involved are familiar with the court and its proceedings, but the other contributing members, such as the gardaí, are not. If a case is to be heard fairly, the gardaí presenting the case must be able to do so effectively and confidently. I always had great sympathy with the gardaí in this regard. In the District Court, as the offences are generally on the lower end of the scale, it tends to be junior gardaí involved in the prosecution. I remember well my own early days as a solicitor in the civil courts, when I was routinely terrified and unsure. I could see the same terror on the faces of the young gardaí in Kilmainham, who might be experiencing a court setting for the first time. I made it my business to say something to put them at their ease and let them know the court wasn't adversarial. We were all there for the same reason: to listen to the case and to ensure that the best and fairest judgment was made on it.

Sometimes a young garda would come to see me beforehand, to ask about the court's procedures – although they never mentioned specifics of the case, and I wouldn't have allowed them to do so – and I always gave them five minutes of my time to answer their questions. I felt it was important that they could perform their duty as well as possible. I found them all wonderful, but youth is youth, and you have a certain way of thinking in your youth that becomes more refined as you get older. You are inexperienced, naturally, and you don't have the same level of nuanced understanding or empathy. And in court, there is so much to attend to as a garda – their own reactions and nervousness, but also the victim's feelings. This was why I welcomed the advent of victim support groups, because I could see that these junior gardaí couldn't support the victims fully. And I also welcomed the EU-led changes that saw victim support units set up in each garda district, which liaise with all the support organisations. Those additions are excellent, but there is still a long way to go to ensure a fair and equal justice system.

Of all the occupations within the court, I always believed, and still do, that the gardaí have the toughest job. They have to run towards situations the rest of us run away from, usually without any idea as to what will happen or how the people involved will react. That fear and uncertainty would undo me. I simply couldn't do their job. Indeed, I have attended the funerals of gardaí who died by suicide in the face of the stress they were experiencing. I've also spoken with gardaí who required counselling after witnessing particularly appalling crimes, such as the 'House of Horrors' case in Roscommon, which involved the rape and abuse of six children by their parents. It just goes to show that the gardaí need support, too.

One way I felt I could offer practical and useful support was by taking part in the legal training offered to garda recruits by the 'mock courts'. I was first invited to participate in 1986, and I continued to be involved until 2008. I see this as an extremely important part of their training, since it contributes to the level playing field I'm describing. It wasn't a paying gig, but I felt privileged to be asked to serve as the presiding mock judge of the mock court. While I was working in Kilmainham, we used the courthouse there as our setting, so the young gardaí became familiar with a proper court set-up. After I retired in 2002, we used various garda locations in Dublin to serve as our courtroom.

The standard of legal training was not high, and when tracking forms (explained below) were brought in, the standard dropped further still. I remember one garda recruit who was undergoing court training, overseen by a panel of senior gardaí. I was in my place in the judge's chair, and a mock witness was brought in and took their place in the box. Back then in the District Court, it was the norm for a garda to take their witness through their evidence, so this was a necessary skill to have.

So, the garda was asked to prove her case. Silence. I said nothing. The gardaí on the panel said nothing. Eventually, one of the gardaí said to the recruit,

'Why aren't you examining the witness?' She looked startled and replied, 'I didn't know I had to.' There ended up being tears and upset, because she was so discombobulated. I was looking at this and thinking to myself, *How could she come out of Templemore with so little knowledge of the court's proceedings?*

An Garda recruits receive their initial court training in Templemore, where they have a beautiful courtroom. I regarded that courtroom with great envy when I saw it and would have given my eye teeth for it, given that Kilmainham was being held up largely by scaffolding and prayers by the time I retired. On one occasion, after I retired, I was invited to visit Templemore with a group of other people. I went as the representative of the National Crime Victims Helpline, along with Maeve Ryan. We were shown around, and when I spotted some gardaí I knew, I enquired as to which garda was in charge of the court training for recruits. I was given the name – it wasn't a garda I had ever met or heard of – and I made it my mission to seek him out. I thought a frank discussion about the standard of training would be welcome, and I certainly regarded it as necessary for all concerned. When I found him, I launched into a very direct assessment of the level of court knowledge I was encountering in the mock courts up in Dublin. And I told him straight that I felt the standard of legal training was very poor, judging by what I saw of the gardaí in the real courtroom at Kilmainham. But it wasn't the open and constructive dialogue I was hoping to have. From what I could see, there was no will to change there. He was more of an academic than a frontline officer, and he had never arrested anyone in the course of his career, so we were coming at it from two very different viewpoints. It was a pity as it was a wasted opportunity.

There has been another innovation that I disagree with, which is the tracking form. This was introduced a few years before my retirement, and I think it's a terrible idea. Before this, when a garda made an arrest, that same garda attended the court when the case was first heard, so that they were present for every stage of the proceedings, rather than simply to prosecute the hearing. This might have been daunting at first, but it gave the garda solid first-hand experience of a court and its proceedings, and over time they became more effective at presenting their cases. Now, the arresting garda fills in a tracking form, and it is the form that appears in court, not the garda. The form is handed to the judge by the court presenter (a new role created since the introduction of tracking forms), and the case is remanded. The accused and their solicitor are present in court, but the prosecuting garda is not. I remember a chap in the dock said to me, 'I want a strike out because the garda is not here.' I said to him, 'If I have to deal with a form, you do too.' But in truth, I wanted to go down and hug him, because he was absolutely right.

The tracking form might save money and garda time, but it's a false economy in my view. It removes the gardaí from the court and deprives them of the knowledge and experience that come from witnessing the end result of their efforts. It also robs them of the ability to build up a reliable working knowledge of the crime fraternity operating in their own and other garda districts. When I was on the bench in Kilmainham, the gardaí could identify which district a chap hailed from by sight alone, because they had a whole rogues' gallery in their heads to draw on. This was down to the fact that they spent time in court, observing who was there, who was loitering, the defendants other gardaí were bringing in – it gave them invaluable insight and information that arguably enabled them to do their jobs better. But this direct knowledge was lost once the gardaí were left out of the courtroom.

One of the worst effects of this change is that the case might be sent forward to the Circuit or other court, which means the higher courts will be the prosecuting garda's first court experience. This is very wrong. The higher courts have a more formal set-up, all those wigs and gowns, plus a jury and myriad other parties involved. The barristers behave in a more intimidating fashion, and it's far more adversarial. A defence barrister is acting for their client and not on behalf of the witnesses. For a junior garda new to the process, it would be all too easy to be unseated by the atmosphere and theatrics of the higher courts. And it affects the course of justice if the garda can't present the case well. For these reasons, I see tracking forms as a retrograde step. It robs the young gardaí of the opportunity to build up court experience, understanding and empathy – and justice will be the poorer for that.

I witnessed this exact problem in Kilmainham before I retired. I had already let it be known that I felt the court training for garda recruits was woefully inadequate, and I had this opinion confirmed in my court on a regular basis. This particular incident really illustrated the repercussions of tracking forms – and it made me hopping mad.

There were two chaps in the dock, facing a charge of stealing a car. They had entered a not guilty plea, so the prosecuting garda was in attendance to present the case against them. The garda informed me that he would also represent the case of a colleague who could not be present, which should be remanded. That was all well and good. He told me that he wanted to press his case that day and that he was fully ready to do so. I'm looking down at the court and I can see his two accused, but no witnesses. Problem. I repeatedly questioned the garda's decision, trying to get him to see the problem, but to no avail. I asked him where his witnesses were. 'I don't need any,' he replied confidently. 'I saw it happening.' I tried to come at it obliquely from different angles, but the penny was not dropping – he kept insisting on the case being heard right then and there. What I was trying to get across to him through my questions was the fact that the hearing required at least the owner of the car as a witness, to tell the court that they had not given their permission to the two lads to take the vehicle. Without that vital piece of evidence, the garda was racing directly towards failure, eyes wide open but seeing nothing.

It was utterly aggravating, and I could feel my blood starting to boil as the garda batted away my questions. He missed the entire point of his presence there and showed himself to have scant knowledge of court proceedings – knowledge so scant, he was about to lose his own case. I tried everything I could within the limits of my role to get him to remand both cases, but he blithely refused. It was a scandalous lack of awareness and understanding, and I was silently cursing the elegant courtroom down in Templemore for its lack of utility. The solicitor for the two chaps knew what I was up to and was watching on with possibly some amusement at my predicament. Indeed, I'd say the two defendants were so savvy about court proceedings that they could see exactly what was going on as well. Everyone but the prosecuting garda could see where this was headed.

Inevitably, I had to dismiss the case. I didn't want both cases to be lost, so I struck out the second one, which would allow his colleague to bring it to court again. But the garda's own case simply could not succeed as presented. The lads congratulated each other, almost in disbelief, I'd say, and then happily walked out of Kilmainham as free men. To my mind, that was a direct consequence of tracking forms and how they denied young gardaí court experience and learning. That garda was the victim of his own ignorance, and he paid dearly for it – of course, society pays dearly for it too, which is the real issue. By the end of my time on the bench, I was disillusioned by the tracking form and its effects. The court did not operate as well, the gardaí did not perform their jobs as well, and that meant I, as judge, could not perform my job as well either. We all lost the daily contacts that had allowed us to learn about each other – judge, garda and criminal – and that meant a huge amount of valuable knowledge leaked out of the gaping hole left in the system by those blasted tracking forms. I would do away with them in a heartbeat, if it were up to me.

Both An Garda and the court system are set up as a hierarchy, which can also bring its own problems. I thoroughly dislike the old idea of respect being a right and judges always being correct. I stand by respect for the authority of the office, but that authority was vested in me as judge – it did not belong to me personally. I would have hated to wear a wig, for example. I did wear a black robe, but I would happily have sat on the bench without it, as it made no difference. I didn't need props to do what I did. I often said to a fella in the dock, 'I can give you six months with or without a smile, no extra charge.' What I meant was that how I looked, how I dressed, who I was... none of that mattered, because the authority existed beyond and above me. I was only ever an instrument.

That attitude was not shared by all of my colleagues. In my earlier days, in particular, judges seemed to live in a Dublin 4 bubble that was very comfortable for them and very male-dominated, and they exuded an air of 'I'm the judge and I'm right'. The hierarchical structure was, of course, fertile ground for the old boys' network to grow and flourish. I have to hold my hand up and say again that my own appointment was helped along by my connection to Gemma Hussey TD, but I always disliked that old boys' mentality because it bred a sense of entitlement, which is dangerous to justice. And what really got to me was that it reached so widely that it threatened to create inappropriate links between the political and judicial spheres, which is something I have always been very, very careful to avoid. Before my own appointment, I was secretary of the Donnybrook branch of Fine Gael, but I severed all ties with the political sphere when I was put on the bench. I immediately resigned as secretary, and I never had any party contact me in all my years, which is as it should be.

However, in my lifetime there has certainly always been a connection between the two spheres. Take my own uncle, for example: his practice was Hussey & O'Higgins, the latter being the famous political family. The link was there from the start, but that doesn't mean we should continue to allow it to exist.

It is important to have a separate and independent judiciary precisely to avoid a network that favours some appointees and mitigates against others. Shane Ross TD argued for the judicial council to comprise a mix of members, including non-legal people. This would seem to be a good idea. This is not to say that there is anything wrong with the appointments made to date, but there might be others out there who are just as capable but can't avail themselves of the opportunity to progress. I think any measure that reinforces the fact that judges are ordinary, decent men and women doing a particular job is a good thing. It has certainly been the case that the old boys' network went against that, which is why I'd hope to see it fully disbanded in my lifetime. I've observed it for decades now, and it is at best unhelpful, at worst exclusive and blinkered. You can't have a level playing field if the referee thinks he is a cut above everyone else on the pitch.

There was one particular incident in my courtroom that brought home to me the dangers and potential adverse consequences of judges having any sense of being above the law. It came about in stages. In the first stage, I dealt with the case of a young jockey who sought to exchange his Mercedes car for a smaller car, with cash being the balance. He carried out this transaction with a reputable car dealer, but it later transpired that his original car was still under an incomplete hire-purchase agreement. The car dealer reported the matter, which was investigated by the fraud squad. In October 1991, the jockey was brought before me at Kilmainham, charged with larceny, false pretences and handling a stolen cheque, as reported in the *Irish Press* on 22 May 1992. I gave him bail and a date in January 1992 for a remand.

When the date arrived, he didn't show up in court, so I issued a bench warrant for his arrest. When he finally did come to court, along with his solicitor, I threatened to put him in custody for non-appearance. However, a friend went bail for him, and the jockey left court on bail for the next remand date. I again remanded the case for service of a Book of Evidence. At the next remand, the young jockey appeared again with his solicitor and the Book of Evidence was still not ready. The solicitor told the court, 'I was assured that the matter would be disposed of this morning.' I recall thinking to myself that this was a very unusual statement to make, as if he had knowledge of something occurring in the background. I again remanded the case. On the remand date, the young jockey once again failed to show up in court. The Book of Evidence was furnished at a further remand date and remanded again, but on the next date the accused once more failed to appear.

Finally, late on a Friday afternoon in May 1992, the jockey and his solicitor put in an appearance at last, along with the prosecuting garda and, unusually at this stage in the proceedings, a barrister for the state. The prosecuting garda was a young man, Detective Garda Feargal Foley, who was to my knowledge the first qualified accountant to join An Garda and become a member of the fraud squad. Straight off the bat, the barrister requested a three-week remand, which was an unusual request. Surprised, I asked, 'Why three weeks?' He replied that he had been instructed to ask for three weeks. I looked at him and said, 'And did you not think to ask why?' No answer. I put the same question to the defence solicitor, who said he did not know why, either.

So I turned to the young garda and asked him if he knew why a three-week remand was being requested. I could sense that he was nervous and reluctant. He outlined that he had received directions from the DPP to prosecute on indictment (that the allegations were deemed to be serious and were to be dealt with in the Circuit Court) in November 1991. He further stated that representations had been made to the DPP, that he had addressed the matters raised and had supplied further evidence to the DPP. He said that he believed representations were being made to the DPP regarding the case by an unnamed third party who had no legal standing in the case, which was 'highly irregular'. I wasn't bothered with that and said to him, 'I don't care who is making recommendations to whom, that's nothing to do with me.' I remanded the young jockey in custody as he had failed to appear in court twice previously. The remand was with consent to bail on the lodgement of £3,000 in cash. I was told the cash was available in the courtroom, which was also unusual. I told him I'd have to dust off his Book of Evidence since it had been lying there so long, waiting for his return.

The next day, I was at home when the phone rang. It was about midday. The voice on the other end said, 'Oh Gillian, this is so-and-so.' I had never met this judge in person, but I knew of him because he was very senior in the legal ranks. I was taken aback that he was calling me – and that he had my home phone number. He said to me, 'I just wanted to tell you that I'm the person making representations to the DPP.' I replied, 'Your secret is safe with me,' but under my breath I said, 'You fool.'

The reason I saw this contact as foolish was because this judge, who was retired at this stage, was interfering in a live case. In doing so, he was reaching far beyond his powers and potentially interfering in the course of justice. What I deduced from this was that he had been approached by someone – he never indicated who – and asked to intervene on behalf of the young jockey. He had evidently agreed to do so, hence the admission that he was in some way petitioning the DPP, recommending perhaps that the case be dropped or other information taken into account. I didn't know any details beyond what he said in that phone call, but my mind was whirring with the possibilities and the potential consequences.

I disagreed with his stance. I had never made such a representations in my career, and I never would. Indeed, I'd no more intervene in such manner than I would fly. I didn't know the full story, but as far as I was concerned, the whole thing stank, and I wondered what would happen next.

That night, I was at a fundraising function run by a member of An Garda. A high-ranking garda was sitting near me, and he remarked, 'You had a bad day in court yesterday.' I said quietly, 'Nothing compared to what I had today.' To this day, I don't know if he heard that comment, but he made no reply at any rate.

The following Friday, we reconvened again: the jockey in the dock, the solicitor and the barrister for the state, and the case was to be sent forward to the Circuit Court. However, the prosecuting garda was not allowed into the witness box. Proceedings got under way, and on three separate occasions the barrister said to me, 'I've been asked to tell you that there are no representations being made to the DPP.' After his third utterance of this, I said, 'I heard you the first time, the second time and the third time. It doesn't matter to me about representations as that is nothing to do with me.' I sent the accused forward for trial to the Circuit Court.

The Sunday after I had received the phone call from the person making representations to the DPP, I was at home when the doorbell rang. I opened the door and there, on the step, stood Detective Garda Foley and his wife. They were both crying. I was a bit stunned by their appearance, but I didn't utter a word other than to invite them inside. I listened as they told me that the young garda had been transferred to uniform duties and that an investigation had been ordered into how he came into possession of incriminating documents, presumably based on the fact that he had mentioned the representations being made to the DPP. I still didn't have the full picture of what was going on here, so I held my own counsel and didn't mention the phone call I'd received. I let them do the talking and I listened carefully.

Foley showed me that he had a copy of these famous documents sent to the DPP, including the one from the retired Judge, but I didn't take them or read them. I simply registered the fact that they did exist, so I knew he was telling the truth. Then he said, 'I'm going to sue the state. Will you support me?' I said I would. What had happened to this young man was not right, and I didn't mind showing him solidarity in the face of such shameful behaviour.

True to his word, the young garda took a case to the High Court, and four years later he contacted me to say the case was being heard in five days' time. I organised the day off work and told no one where I was going. Between the judge's phone call on that Saturday and the case being heard four years later, I had never breathed a word of that phone call to a living soul. The first time I did so was when I met Foley's barrister. I said to him, 'You're the first person I've told, but I don't know how we'll get this into my evidence in the witness box.' He didn't know either.

The hearing took place on a beautiful sunny Wednesday in October 1996, and I was scheduled to give evidence in the afternoon. When the session commenced, I was called first, and the questioning began. It was a very unreal situation for me, to be appearing as a witness in the High Court. I couldn't recall hearing of any other judge who had done this. But I kept my wits about me. The barrister suggested very strongly to me that Garda Foley had volunteered these 'allegations to the court'. I told the barrister that was incorrect, that he was reluctant and that 'I had to prise it out of him'. I then managed to slip in the fact that I had received a phone call about the representations and the three-week remand. The barrister immediately countered with, 'You can't name the caller.' I replied that I had no intention of doing so, but I knew that I had planted a seed.

The next day, I was back at work in Kilmainham, and at lunchtime I had two widely smiling visitors: the young garda and his wife. His case had been settled. I was so glad and relieved. That episode could have ruined his career, but he went on to become an inspector. However, the whole thing left a sour taste in his mouth – and mine. When I had asked in court about the reason for the three-week remand, had any of them lied to me? And why did I receive that phone call? I can't answer that for certain, but it felt completely wrong to me. It all beggared belief, and I felt angry at the legal colleague who had tried to influence a hearing in my court based simply on the fact that he had a social connection to the defendant, and also at the gardaí who had turned on their young colleague when all he did was tell the truth.

Those sorts of incidents are very difficult because, as a judge, you are isolated. I couldn't speak to anyone about it. And then I couldn't say anything about the phone call in open court because it was hearsay and therefore inadmissible. It was very stressful, having to hold my own counsel all the time. But I was glad I was able to stand by the young garda, and I admired him for taking the action and insisting that the law be applied equally to all. It was a very nasty experience for him, too.

This is why I was always wary of judges who let the power go to their heads and who began to see themselves as the site of justice. That's dangerous thinking. For my own part, the only time I was ever approached by the political sphere was early one November, after another nightmarish Halloween in Ballyfermot. There were always casualties on that night, and sometimes even deaths. After one particularly awful year, when two children were badly burned at a bonfire, I received an unexpected call from the Department of Justice. I was very surprised, as it was the first such call I had ever received in my career. I didn't know it then, but it would also be the last. The official who rang me asked if I had any ideas for a programme to put in place in Ballyfermot to tackle the Halloween madness. I replied, 'Would you please contact the chief super in Ballyfermot Garda Station, because he's been trying to do exactly this for several years with no assistance whatsoever?' Later, that programme was put in place, so I guess the DoJ official must have taken my advice.

That was my closest contact with the political sphere in my capacity as judge. I was extremely aware of the need to maintain a distance from politicians and stuck to that for my whole career. It is imperative that judges don't come to view themselves as some sort of ruling class. That's not their function at all. The Irish State is explicitly founded on the separation of powers. The Constitution established the Legislature, the Executive and the Judiciary, and these three entities are intended to function without interfering with each other. The courts exercise the judicial power of the Irish Government and must do so independently. As I recounted earlier, at our swearing-in ceremony, all new judges take an oath to 'be independent in the exercise of their judicial functions and subject only to this Constitution and the law'. That is the basis of the entire justice system, and it must be protected. Every judge must work to uphold that founding principle.

Recently, I came across a very interesting book called *The Irish District Court: A Social Portrait*.[*] When I first read it, I was absolutely furious. It presented a story of judges acting on whims, an allegation that greatly offended me. The author noted that the 'punishment meted out ... may depend on the character and humour of the presiding judge'. I'd hate people to think that of me and my work on the bench, and it upset me enormously to see it written in black and white. But then I spoke to an old friend and former probation officer, Anna Rynn. I described the thrust of the book's argument to her, and she was completely unfazed. She said, 'You weren't like that, but others were. The power went to their heads. A bad night's sleep could

_____

[*] *The Irish District Court: A Social Portrait*, Caroline O'Nolan (Cork University Press, 2013)

affect their decisions.' That rocked me back on my heels. I sat and thought it over, and I realised that Anna was right: the book wasn't inaccurate in its portrayal, although it didn't by any means apply to every judge. I could, however, think of three or four judges to whom I felt it would apply. Of course, that didn't change the fact that I hated being tarred with the same brush.

That portrayal was tapping into the seam of entitlement that used to run through the judiciary. It was literally a boys' club, because there were so few women in the profession back then. Barristers got cases through personal contacts, which naturally favoured those who had attended certain schools and colleges. That made it difficult for women to break down the door. But we did. In 2021 I met a friend for coffee who was studying with the Law Society of Ireland at Blackhall Place and she told me there were about 430 students in her class, with more women than men. That was astounding to me, because it's so markedly different from my own student experience. But it shows that the legal profession has changed utterly and, I would argue, for the better of all.

It has long been the case that studying law is a costly undertaking, requiring financial resources that are well beyond most people. This must be tackled further, but I was heartened to learn about the Public Access to Law (PAL) programme being run in secondary schools. The aim is to pull back the curtain and make the courts and their proceedings more visible and more accessible. It is to be hoped that initiatives of this sort open up the possibility of studying law to a much wider cohort. Years ago, the Bar was shrouded in mystery, and only the expensively initiated were allowed near it. This is at the root of the problem with the judicial system, so I'm glad to see it finally being weeded out. This progress should herald the end of the old boys' network.

The only way for a court to be an effective network of viable solutions is to achieve a level playing field – in other words, respect between all the parties. It is true that ultimate responsibility for delivering justice rests on the judge's shoulders, but if that responsibility is borne within an equitable, decent and fair court, then I think that places the judge in the best position to make good judgments. But the respect must lie primarily with the institution and its power to make a difference, and the judge must understand their role in this regard. We are, after all, afforded the right to be judged by our peers, not by our betters.

The judicial system is undergoing change, but more is needed to ensure it is an open, transparent and fair system at every level. There was no training for judges in my day, though it was brought in a few years after I went on the bench. The method then was to assign a new judge to a veteran judge, so that the new appointee could observe and learn. However, thanks to *The Irish District Court* book, I'm now wondering what those novices actually learned. That style of training depends entirely on the teacher, which might prove successful or might not. In fact, I recall a registrar once marvelling at the veteran judge chosen to train the new gowns and muttering, 'They'll learn nothing from him.'

Like the gardaí, judges must receive ongoing training to enable them to deal effectively with all the crimes that come before them, particularly sexual and domestic violence offences, and also the new offences of the digital age, like cybercrime. It's not possible to turn up and hear cases like this off the cuff. It is essential that all those involved in delivering justice are trained and knowledgeable. I also believe that the very best workplaces have a strong mix of gender and age. That way, you harness the best of everything. I think it is all going in the right direction, which is reassuring. I look forward to seeing ordinary, decent judges who operate a justice system that is fair and equal in its scope and approach and that continues to adhere to the highest ethical principles. It is what any civilised society deserves – indeed, it is what it can be judged by.

CHAPTER 11

LET JUSTICE BE DONE THOUGH THE HEAVENS FALL

One of the most memorable days in Kilmainham District Court was the day the three men accused of the Veronica Guerin murder were brought before the bench. There was great activity in the court, with enhanced security – although not as much security as for Derry O'Rourke, I noted. The mere fact that these three men were present in the District Court was big news. They wouldn't have been District Court material, given the level of their criminal ambitions, so they

CHAPTER 11

were a rare sighting in this jurisdiction. That didn't affect me, though. My routine and approach didn't change, although obviously I was aware that there was a more serious and more sinister atmosphere in the courtroom. Otherwise, I simply got on with the job in hand.

Veronica Guerin was a fearless investigative reporter, of the kind that filled you with admiration and anxiety in equal measure. I often wondered if her age – just 37 years old when she was killed – made her braver than most. But I admired her very much. I met her once, at a social function, and I was impressed by the fact that she was 'on' at all times. She put questions to me and was intensely focused on her work, even on what was meant to be a night off. It was clear that her work was all-important and that she was striving to do it well.

On the day of her murder, Wednesday, 26 June 1996, I had lunch in Parliament Street and then returned to Kilmainham for the afternoon session. When I got there, the place was abuzz, and I was soon told the reason why: Veronica had been shot dead in her car on the M7. Assassinated. There was a real sense of people being on edge around

269

the court, a sense that this could herald a new and dangerous chapter for all of us. It was the first killing of a journalist in Ireland, and the shockwaves reverberated in every corner of society, but especially across the gardaí and the criminal justice system.

That day and in the days that followed, I heard different attitudes to Veronica and her death. Some people expressed admiration for her tenacity, but there was a seam of criticism as well. There were some who said she brought it on herself, that she pushed too hard and it was an inevitable outcome. I felt that response was based on misogyny, because I didn't think they would have said that of a male journalist. I also remembered that no one had batted an eyelid when she was shot in the leg and when she was assaulted by John Gilligan. There had been no voices raised in criticism or concern, then. So I didn't allow those comments in my company. I thought she was very brave and did the country a huge service. Her work and her death led to the setting up of the Criminal Assets Bureau, which is a hefty legacy. Veronica did a lot for all of us in her short life.

When the case came to Kilmainham, there were three men in the dock: Patrick 'Dutchy' Holland,

Charles Bowden and Paul Ward. The court's security was beefed up by the presence of the Emergency Response Unit and Special Branch detectives, although I wouldn't have noticed them as they kept a low profile. But they had to be there, because there were credible threats to the gang members if they cooperated, so the gardaí had to tread very carefully. That level of security was unusual at Kilmainham, although it would have been par for the course at the Special Criminal Court, so that added a frisson of excitement to the proceedings. On that first outing, I remanded the men in custody for the Book of Evidence to be prepared.

They returned to court for several remands until the Book of Evidence was served, and I was satisfied that they should be sent forward for trial. That was the extent of my involvement in the case. That District Court hearing put those men in the criminal justice system, which no doubt prompted a sigh of relief from the gardaí and the general public. There was a funny moment, though, one that left the gardaí red-faced and me shocked, but suppressing a smile. I returned to the court after my lunch break, only to be met by the sight of a couple in a passionate clinch. Charles Bowden's girlfriend had come to support him, and a kind garda had allowed her to approach him to say a quick hello. Although this was the one and only time I witnessed such a scene, I've learned since then from talking to retired gardaí that it wasn't entirely unusual in the District Court. Since many of the crimes were minor, the gardaí were decent towards the defendants, sometimes allowing their parents, siblings or partners to have a quick hug and a word with them. There's a humanity to that approach that I appreciate. On this occasion, though, the gardaí were absolutely mortified that I had to walk past the kissing couple on my way to the bench. That most certainly was unusual! The gardaí always observed the decorum of the court, so a breach of that nature was rare.

We were all more careful with regard to our personal security after Veronica's death. I was well aware that I wasn't flavour of the month with these people, so it was a slightly nerve-racking time. However, the state response was swift and robust, so thankfully no one else was injured or murdered. Assistant Commissioner Tony Hickey led that investigation, and at his retirement party in March 2005 I was introduced to Bernie Guerin, Veronica's mother. She was a great character, and we really clicked. After that, we met once a month in the Gresham Hotel for a chat. She was a wonderful person who carried her grief with dignity and forbearance.

Bernie died on 15 January 2014, and I lost a friend and favourite lunch companion. I couldn't attend her funeral because I was speaking in the Senate that day, alongside Detective Superintendent Noel Clarke. This was a first for the Senate: a retired judge and a garda addressing various members on the subject of the criminal world and drugs. Our aim was to enlighten the senators as to the reality on the ground being faced by terrified communities around the country. I was absolutely petrified doing that talk, which will likely surprise people to hear. I find any kind of public speaking intimidating and pay a heavy personal toll every time I do it. That might sound odd for a judge who presides over a courtroom in a very public way, but the court was my office, so I was comfortable there. Once outside that office, however, I was shy and happy to live in the shadows as much as possible. Garda Liam Hogan once remarked to me, 'Of course, you're very shy.' I beamed at him and said, 'I want to throw my arms around you, because you're the only one who's ever seen it.' He was, and is, a very astute man.

Aside from that very high-profile case, the schedule of daily cases at Kilmainham remained extremely busy and extremely diverse. We were seeing more sexual offences cases, unfortunately, and it was striking how many of them involved alcohol. I remember one case that stood out because I felt the accused was being dealt with incorrectly. It involved a teenager who worked as a barman at weekends. There was a customer who drank steadily in the bar every Saturday, spending hours there. This customer was in his forties and had recently remarried. This particular Saturday, he sexually assaulted the young barman, who reported it. And so it came before me to hear both sides.

The young victim was very upset, but his parents were distraught. They appeared angry and aggressive in court, and they wanted a prison sentence straightaway, no questions asked. I felt there was addiction at work here, and potentially a hidden sexual identity, so I requested a probation report for the accused. When it arrived, it was a glowing report, with no mention whatsoever of alcoholism or sexuality. That struck me as strange – and incomplete. It wasn't my job to assess the man or compile the report, but it bothered me that the counsellor appeared to have missed a large part of the problem.

When the case came back before me on a further remand, with the report in hand from the accused's counsellor, I had no option but to give a custodial sentence, given that the counsellor had failed to hit the nail on the head. However, I took the unusual step of saying privately to the accused's barrister and solicitor that I felt he ought to secure a new counsellor. That was all I could do in that situation: give the man the sharp shock of prison, and quietly tell his team that he appeared to be wasting his money on that particular counsellor. I had also quietly made inquiries of the garda and probation officer involved, and they confirmed that the accused did have a drinking problem. They could see it, I could see it, but unfortunately the person paid to notice it was blind to it. Even so, I recommended to the parents of the boy that they seek counselling too, to cope with their deep-seated anger, but they refused. I felt that was a very sad and unsatisfactory case for everyone concerned.

There were so many crimes linked to alcohol consumption. One of the most common involved the young men who were arrested late at night and charged with breach of the peace or drunk and disorderly. Typically, these fellows had no previous interaction with the gardaí and would arrive into the court, with their father, solicitor and various family members, looking sheepish and embarrassed. These, at least, were easy cases to solve. I had a tried and trusted method at my disposal: the court poor box. I had my own approach to using the poor box, which was actually located in the Bridewell, though I created a highly functioning Kilmainham branch. I had used it first in the case of Phil Lynott, when he was before me in the Bridewell on a charge of drug possession. I asked him to donate £5,000 to the poor box, and I divided the money between two charities.

Once I saw those sheepish young men come through the door, I would be thinking of the benefit to the poor box. These men were first-time offenders on a minor charge, and the possibility of reoffending or progressing on to higher-level offences was extremely low. The presence of the family members in court and the general air of deep contrition made that clear. So I'd suggest a donation, and the young man would nearly swoon with gratitude and relief. I saw to it that all such funds were immediately donated to local organisations in the area where the crime had been committed. I chose organisations that didn't receive much help or funding, like the Kevin Street Youth Diversion Programme. I had an excellent ally in DI Gerry Lovett of Kevin Street Garda Station, who was familiar with all such organisations in his jurisdiction. I remember sending money to a breakfast club in St Michael's Estate and receiving a beautiful letter of thanks in return. I was taken aback by their appreciation – it was humbling.

I think my approach might have been frowned upon down at the Bridewell, but I never canvassed opinion on it. I was familiar with the poor box at the Bridewell from my early days on the bench. The chief clerk there had invited me one day and asked me if I would distribute the poor box money to worthy recipients. I've no idea why he chose me for this task, but I gladly tackled it. When I counted the money, it ran to a few thousand pounds, which I thought was scandalous, that it was sitting there, unused and doing nothing. That never happened in Kilmainham – the poor box money was distributed as soon as it was received. That said, I wasn't a prolific user of that option. I was never christened 'the poor box judge', as some were. There were only certain types of situation and person I deemed eligible for this treatment, but it was a handy option to have when it was suitable.

In the late 1990s, a new issue began to take up a lot of court time and resources, much to my despair. That is when we began to see a large number of defendants who did not speak English and about whom very little was known beyond the bare facts of what had landed them in court. It got to the point where about a third of court appearances featured immigrants of many different nationalities, and I despaired because it was impossible to deliver to them the type of justice I wished to deliver. It was extremely difficult for everyone involved in the Courts Service and ancillary services, and it put a real strain on the system.

The language barrier posed a huge problem. It meant interpreters had to be used in court, which in turn meant that I was relying on the honesty and accuracy of the interpreter in order to understand what had happened and why. As a result, I had to take the interpreter's word at face value, which didn't always sit well with me. The offences were usually minor, like begging or being a public nuisance at traffic lights and the like. A typical scenario would involve a person who was living in a hostel and signing on for the dole. They might get frustrated in the dole office (probably the language barrier again), they might gesticulate in a manner deemed aggressive or raise their voice, and the next thing the gardaí would be called to shift them. Then they were brought to court for these petty crimes, and the whole place was tied up in knots trying to establish basic communication to meet their needs and rights. My choices were severely limited, because they couldn't engage properly with the Probation Service, but at the same time I knew that custody was a poor solution. It was really difficult because it undid my whole philosophy of the court and its function by tying my hands with regard to alternatives to prison.

I saw many Romanian people come through the court, and I found them very interesting. The women would be sent out to beg, but if they were arrested, there would be a row of men at the back of the court to support them. Whenever bail was granted, a wad of notes would emerge from trouser pockets and be passed up to the registrar – incredible amounts. As a woman judge, I realised that they often thought I'd be a soft touch. I remember two men who were arrested for trying to steal money at an ATM. A person was removing their cash from the machine when these two men put their hands on him, only to have the two plain-clothes gardaí behind them place their hands firmly on their shoulders. So here they were in court: one was tall and heavily built, the other smaller. The smaller chap told me he was 14 years old. I looked at him and said, 'Do you have a birth cert?' He said no, and the interpreter backed him up on the implausible age he was claiming. I said to him, 'You must have been born with a razor in your pocket', since he looked old enough to have been shaving for several years. I put them both in custody, in the adult prison.

I really disliked those cases and how we had to deal with them. It was an issue that arose very suddenly, and the gardaí, courts and prison service simply weren't prepared for it. But at least I was able to do more productive work in that regard after I retired, when I joined the tribunal that heard appeals lodged by asylum seekers in Ireland. I did that once a week for a year, examining appeals and trying to establish the veracity of people's claims. There was one particular case where the applicant had previously been put in custody by a District Court and made his application for citizenship while in custody. I had read all the documents, but I had to go to his solicitor and ask if he had appeared before me in Kilmainham, given that the District Court in question wasn't named in the documents. I explained that if that was the case, he would be entitled to seek someone else to assess his appeal. In the end, the case proceeded under my care, and the applicant was granted leave to stay. Afterwards, when I was in my room, there was a soft knock on the door. It was the interpreter who had assisted the proceedings. I invited him in, and he told me that the chap's claim as to his home country was likely a lie because his accent wasn't of that region. I listened, but I didn't change my decision. The judgment had been made and the papers filed. Based on all the available information, the man no doubt needed the help the country was prepared to offer him. Plus, I felt it would be extremely difficult to prove categorically that his claimed place of birth was untrue. It just goes to show how much of an obstacle the language barrier is in such circumstances – and also that my gut instinct about the veracity of some claims was correct.

There was another new development that seemed like a curse at first but soon proved to be a blessing in disguise. In 1998, I was diagnosed with rheumatoid arthritis, which robbed me of my ability to write. As a judge, you take notes constantly, so I couldn't do my job properly and was facing the prospect of being forced to resign early. After my diagnosis, I ended up in Peamount Hospital and missed 11 months of work. However, during that time, I attended a District Court conference and asked about the possibility of a laptop and of developing a secure program specifically for the use of the judges. We had actually been given laptops around 1996, but no one knew what to do with them. One judge put his in his garden shed, while others handed them over to their grandchildren. There was a complete lack of joined-up thinking on that one. However, I was blessed with a very tech-savvy son, Duncan, who lived in the USA but had left behind in my house a monstrously big PC, with the strict instruction that I was to learn how to use it. I did, struggling away on my own until I'd figured it out. So now it hit me that my newfound skill might be put to good use.

A firm in Blackrock was employed to look into the laptop question. A man came out to Kilmainham to watch the court's proceedings, with a view to figuring out exactly what I needed to do my job. I was on sick leave at that time, due to the arthritis, so I brought him to Kilmainham and let him observe a colleague in action. As a serving judge, I wasn't permitted into another judge's court in session, so I waited for him in the garda office. He observed closely and then went off to design a program to fit the bill.

On Christmas Eve 1999, my doorbell at home rang, and it was this man, bringing me the best

Christmas present ever: a work-ready laptop, specially designed and programmed for my use. I went back to work in January, and he sat in the court for three weeks, to be on hand should problems arise, but none ever did. I was up and running – and it was a revelation. All of my court work and relevant documents were sent from the Four Courts and stored on the laptop, for retrieval at the push of a button. I had my ferocious memory then, of course, but this backup system meant I was invincible. In one case, a garda gave evidence of an arrest made at 3.44 a.m. As I listened, I was musing that the fella in the dock was likely on bail with conditions. With a click of the mouse, I called up his file and saw that I was right. I put him straight into custody on the basis that he had broken his bail conditions, which required him to be at home from 10 p.m. until morning. His solicitor was gobsmacked by the speed with which it all happened.

That laptop put the Four Courts at my fingertips. To this day, not many judges use computers in court, but I would highly recommend it. I was very grateful to my son that his insistence on acquiring IT skills bought me extra time on the bench – and the distinction of being the first judge to use a computer in court. It meant I got four years on the bench I would have otherwise been denied, although the harsh truth was that both I and the building at Kilmainham were nearing the end of our working lives.

One of the things I loved most about working in Kilmainham was the courthouse building itself. It was beautiful, with real character. But by this stage, it was about 180 years old, and its age was showing. I had a spacious, well-appointed chamber that was a joy to work in. Originally, it housed the District Court judge, the registrar and the gardaí, so it felt crowded. A garda would man the phone, but people wishing to visit could ring my phone line to announce themselves and then be brought up to me. When I was sharing the room, the garda working the phone knew exactly who was coming to visit me, meaning that I had no privacy.

Another colleague was working in Kilmainham for a period and using the judge's chamber, and he rang me to say, 'You have to get these people out of the room. It's disgraceful.' I knew he was right, so I made an appointment with the superintendent at Kevin Street Garda Station and went to set out my case to him. We decided that he would drop into the court one day to casually see what was going on, and he would ask the gardaí present why they were in the judge's chamber. He did this, and it quickly transpired that no one could give a terribly good reason for being there. As a result, he asked every garda to hand over their key to the room to me, which they did. I was so glad. I had no privacy whatsoever when the room was being shared, and it was important that I could conduct conversations in person and on the phone in private. By finally demarcating the space for the judge alone, I was clearing up an inherited problem. One of my predecessors had been there a long time, and he had run the chamber in this way. It had become 'the way it's done', which was why some people were reluctant to change it for the newest judge. But it all ended well: the gardaí were given their own room, and then I had that lovely big chamber all to myself.

I loved that chamber, but in the late 1980s/early '90s its age was beginning to show. Structural issues with the old building were making themselves known, and my lovely chamber ended up being held up by scaffolding. The cells were deathly cold, and there was a fungus taking hold throughout the building. We no longer had the level of secure facilities required to bring in people in custody, so the court couldn't function properly. It made me think of the Latin inscription over the entrance to the Bridewell Garda Station: *Fiat Justitia, Ruat Caelum – Let justice be done though the heavens fall.* In the case of Kilmainham, we were trying to keep doing justice even as the building was threatening to fall down around our ears.

One day in early November 1988, I was in my chamber when something moved at the corner of my vision. I had a long table running down the middle of the room, a chair and a dustbin. Something scuttled from the bin to the floor-to-ceiling cupboard that held the Books of Evidence, among many other items and documents. I didn't see it clearly, but I knew it was likely a mouse or a rat. I sought help in the garda room. The gardaí I found there were reluctant to come and hunt for vermin, but eventually one garda came into the chamber and confirmed my fears. As it happened, the chamber had become home to both rats and mice, which is unusual, but apparently the proximity of the River Camac was to blame.

This severe infestation, on top of all the other problems plaguing the building, meant that I was forced to call the president of the District Court and inform him that Kilmainham was no longer fit for purpose. We could not continue. We could deal with cases on remand, but we couldn't hear any cases. The courthouse simply wasn't up to it anymore. That was a big call to make, but there really was no choice. My son Ronan, the newspaper photographer, came up to Kilmainham, took a picture of me on the steps of the courthouse and broke the news that the court was closing. His editor was astonished and asked, 'How do you know that?' He told them, 'I have it from the horse's mouth!'

The problem was, there was no other court in Dublin that was suitable for hearing cases involving prisoners in custody, which required secure cells and so forth, so we were forced to limp on for a few more months. In 1988, we closed two weeks early for the summer recess, and the Office of Public Works took over the building and commenced a programme of restoration works, with a view to patching up the major problems and making the building functional again. When the court resumed in September, we returned to a building that was in a better state, but certainly not in pristine condition.

My beautiful chamber was still out of bounds because it was deemed unsafe, so instead I was put in a tiny shoebox of a room upstairs. Donkey's years before, it had been part of the quarters of the resident magistrate, and it was located on the far side of the building. There was a water tank in the room next door that was frequented by boisterous, raucous pigeons. It was far from comfortable.

I thought this arrangement would be temporary, but it dragged on for years. The building continued to sag gently into old age, and I never got my lovely chamber back. For the next 14 years, I lived cheek by jowl with those pigeons in the unlovely shoebox. The court conducted its business, but the circumstances were not ideal; the heavens still seemed to be determined to fall.

By now, I was 65 years old and had served 18 years on the bench in all. Judges must retire at 70, so I could have gone on for another five years, but I decided against it. There were a number of reasons behind my early retirement. I was paying a large portion of my salary on tax, which was irritating. At that stage in my life, I had no family commitments to offset against salary, so I was in a position where I could afford to retire. But, most of all, I was dissatisfied and disillusioned with the lack of state involvement in dealing with many pressing issues, particularly with regard to mental health services. I am now 20 years retired, writing in 2022, and I could still make that same statement, which is a terrible indictment on successive governments. Within the Courts Service and An Garda, we were doing our jobs as best we could, but our ability and potential were hampered by a lack of support and a lack of vision.

It had also upset and angered me that so many in our prison population seemed not to belong there – that they required help with their mental health, not incarceration. And the real problem was that I simply could not see that changing. We were never approached by anybody from the state's side to investigate these matters, so it felt like we were battling away alone while everyone looked the other way and refused to see what was happening. After a time, it becomes harder and harder to get up every day and do battle once more. When there is no change, and there seems to be no appetite for it, it is deeply disheartening. And that was what happened to me, really. After 16 years of it, I became disheartened by the daily tide of human misery washing through Kilmainham when we had so few resources to make a real difference. Each day, the tide washed out and back in again, bringing more stories of poverty and deprivation and undiagnosed mental health problems that led people to commit criminal acts. I wanted the court to be a vital network, to provide alternatives and strong social justice. That had always been difficult to achieve, and it felt like it was becoming even more challenging. I surveyed my career and my work and my ambitions, and I could no longer ignore the disconnect between them.

There was another factor in my decision, a much more positive one. Although I was feeling disillusioned with the social fabric surrounding the court, I was still heavily involved on the boards of many different organisations that were working towards real change. By retiring from the bench, I would be able to give even more time and energy to the many different projects with which I wanted to be involved. There was Tiglin, of course, and St James's Camino and the National Crime Victims Helpline, for all of which I remain a patron. There was so much work to be done, and they all needed willing volunteers to help. Retirement would free me up to work in those areas where real change might still be possible to achieve.

The decision was made. I had enjoyed almost two decades as a judge, and I cherished that experience. I'd had a wonderful career: challenging, enjoyable, sometimes terrible, often hilarious. I was blessed to have somehow ended up on the bench, and on the bench in the District Court on the criminal side. It was my home all those years, and everyone in it was my family – that's how it felt. I had learned so much, realised so much and come to understand myself so much better through the lessons taught to me by the bench. Now it was time to take that knowledge and experience out into the world beyond the courthouse doors and apply them on the frontline. I was sad to drop the curtain on my career as a judge, but I was very excited to walk outside and down those steps, into whatever was waiting for me there. On 5 April 2002 I retired as a judge of the District Court. Goodbye, Kilmainham.

CHAPTER 12

TIME DELIVERS THE VERDICT
ON YOUR DECISIONS

When you live to old age, as I've been lucky to do, it's extremely interesting to have so much past laid out behind you. It's like standing on a terrace and seeing a whole vista of your life: what you did, what you learned, what you lost or gave up, what you held on to and what finally matters the most. The patchwork patterns of your many decisions over the course of your life are interesting to observe from this distance. It becomes clear that we make decisions in the present, weighing up what evidence we have, using past experience to inform our thinking, but we never can know where that decision will eventually lead and what its end point might be – that's beyond our knowing in any present moment. We make a choice, and we hope it will do no harm and reap dividends – as in life, so in the courtroom.

When I first sat on the criminal bench, I was terrified. I was afraid of everything. I was fearful of the people in the dock, fearful I'd make the wrong decision – the whole experience of my daily work was tinged with fear, which was very uncomfortable. However, looking back, I was perfectly correct to be afraid. For one thing, it was an onerous responsibility to judge the actions and motives of others. There was plenty of scope to make bad decisions as well as good ones. I wasn't a doctor, so it wasn't quite life and death, but it was about liberty and justice, and that meant it was an extremely high level of decision-making with real-world ramifications. I felt the weight of that responsibility very keenly, and it was that understanding that created my fear. I'm glad I had that understanding.

For another thing, that fear demanded that I deal with it, and I did so by pursuing my own education, so that I could do my job to the best of my ability. I had done a course in criminal law as a student in the 1950s, but that was it: the full extent of my dealings on the matter. I had never anticipated doing criminal law at any point, so I hadn't focused on it in any meaningful way. Once I found myself unexpectedly on the criminal bench, I sought help from the probation officers, the registrars and the gardaí, and I looked to learn all I could from the victims and the accused who came before me each day, from their stories and experiences. The change happened gradually, but slowly, over time, I became more comfortable in my job. After some years, I felt completely at home in Kilmainham and on the bench.

I had a strong sense that words could impact people in ways I could never predict and certainly couldn't control. I knew this from my own life, where certain things my father had told me repeatedly – such as his insistence that I wasn't capable of creative thinking – had stuck fast to me. An idea, a phrase, a characterisation can lodge in the brain and stay put for many years, continuing to have an impact long after the words are uttered. We never know which casual comment or unthinking throwaway remark will land and become stuck fast. Words can upset a person deeply, and for a long time. They can be the impetus to change or give rise to a determination not to change. It's a very tricky business. I knew it personally, so I was aware of it professionally. My words carried the weight of my office when I was on the bench, so I did my best to choose them well and carefully, but there was so much I could not know and, indeed, would never know. Our words have a life of their own, beyond us, and we have to accept that as well.

After appearing on *The Tommy Tiernan Show* in 2021, I received some letters of thanks from people who had been in the dock, and otherwise, in Kilmainham. Again, I was struck by where my words had fallen and by the impact they had had. There was a letter from a young woman who thanked me for putting her then boyfriend in custody, thus protecting her from him. She also thanked me for putting Fr Tony Walsh in custody, because it had made a huge difference to friends of hers who had been his victims. I will never cease to be amazed and thankful that I convicted Walsh, even though the odds were stacked against that decision, given that he had a prison officer giving him a cast-iron alibi. But I beat the odds on that occasion, and it was incredible to hear that that decision in my courtroom had rippled out into so many lives beyond its doors. I could never have known, as I handed down his sentence, that it would be felt by so many people across the country. That's astonishing to me, and it makes me feel proud and relieved that my judgment proved sound that day.

Another letter was from a man who had appeared before me in Kilmainham as a young man. He told me I had given him a chance and thanked me for my 'warmth and compassion'. He had never reoffended, had changed his life's track entirely and was now a lecturer on crime and safety, working with law-enforcement agencies around the world. That was quite something to read! I felt a sense of relief flood through me when I read that – I had listened and extended compassion, and those words, those gestures had landed on fertile ground and made a difference. Again, I was so grateful to be allowed the chance to hear the end of that story, after hearing the beginning of it in Kilmainham so many years before. Those are the really good moments as a judge and retired judge.

It's hard to estimate how many decisions went this way and how many didn't have the desired effect, because I only really get to hear about the successes. When I'm at Tiglin or at St James's Camino, or at graduation ceremonies at treatment centres, I'm often approached by people who want to let me know that they took the second chance offered to them by the court services and ran with it. Because they did all the hard work of changing, I get to hear those stories of judgments come good. And I'm always so grateful to know that my court played some small part in delivering the second chance that made the difference. I always tell people that no one is more thrilled and satisfied by their transformation than I am. It's a wonderful feeling to receive a thank you of that nature and to know that a person's life was improved by their brush with the law. I think that's the hallmark of a decent and civilised society.

Again, I'm reminded of young Gillian, whose mother stood in the court and wept for her. Those tears moved me. I related to her not only as a judge, but as a mother. And Gillian was such a little waif of a girl, it made me feel ever sorrier for her mother. It took me years to see and understand that from those tears flowed Tiglin and all the immeasurable good it has done. Those tears impacted on me, I gave young Gillian a second chance, she took that chance and changed her life completely. From that, we were asked to give a talk about our friendship, and from a throwaway remark during that talk, the seed of Tiglin was planted in the mind of Aubrey McCarthy. I still marvel at how it all came about. That woman could never, ever have known that her tears that day would spark a chain reaction that would go on to touch the lives of so many others. Her pleading words also fell on fertile ground, and that extraordinary moment gave rise to so much.

The influence our words can have is frightening as much as inspiring. How many words do we speak in our lives, and how often do we get to fully understand their impact? I remember appearing on *The Late Late Show* in 2018, and I was terrified of sitting on that chair and talking. I was a nervous wreck. But I got through it, and six weeks later I was told of a new resident at a Tiglin treatment centre in Brittas Bay. The chairman of the facility asked her, 'Why did you come here?' And she told him that she had heard a woman on TV speaking about second chances. When the programme had aired, she was too drunk to watch or hear, but her aunts had recorded it and when she was somewhat sober, they had sat her down to watch it. After watching it, she signed up to dry out. I was at that woman's graduation a year later. My words hit home with her because she had the desire to change. If that desire is not there, you may as well save your breath to cool porridge. But if it's there, no matter how deeply buried, the right words can unlock it. It's so interesting to me how our disparate lives are connected in these intangible ways.

For decisions to impact positively and effect change, they must be based on empathy. I've seen this proved again and again. The greatest level of empathy I witnessed in my career was that achieved by John Lonergan, governor of Mountjoy Prison from 1992 to 2010 (after a prior stint as governor from 1984 to 1988). He is an amazing person, and had a unique ability to empathise with the prisoners of Mountjoy and extend a helping hand to them and their families. That level of empathy is very difficult to achieve and to sustain, but John Lonergan managed it. Time will surely deliver a resounding verdict on his career and show that he helped so many people in so many ways. The key to his success was that he showed those men in his care the possibility of a different life. He proved that, with the proper supports, you can change lives.

I have received thanks from people I put in prison, which sounds odd, but sometimes good fortune can come disguised as a spell behind bars. For some, being arrested and imprisoned gives them a new perspective and sometimes a new determination to make different choices. There was one man, an addict, who appeared before me repeatedly, and I repeatedly put him in prison. It was the right decision, because he had no intention of changing, no desire to lead a different life. He was so far gone on drugs, I honestly thought he'd be dead before long. I was wrong, though. He survived. Some years later, he approached me at the launch of a report on suicide in Dublin 8 and asked if I remembered him. I said I did but could not think of his name. He told me his name, and my reply was, 'I thought you would have been dead long ago.' He replied, 'I would have been were it not for you. Can I give you a hug?' I opened my arms and told him to go right on ahead. He said he wanted to thank me for saving his life, that prison had eventually saved him. When he was ready, he chose a different path and was so grateful he had lived to take that opportunity.

There is a lovely postscript to that man's story. A few years ago I was attending an awards ceremony for Meath Street Youth Activity Company. There, to present a soccer award, was an 18-year-old man, a gifted footballer who was being scouted by English clubs. When I heard his name, I asked to meet him. He came over, and I told him that I knew his father, who was the man who had wanted to hug me. It was absolutely wonderful to see that he had produced this tremendous young man, who was living a totally different life from the one his father had lived at his age. There was that chain of events again: the justice system created the conditions whereby the father could save himself, and that, in turn, granted his son a better shot at life. One positive creates so many more.

The decision is obviously the preserve of the judge in the District Court and the crucial moment in any case, so how does a judge arrive at a decision? I've had plenty of time to think about all the things I've learned about justice over the years – especially during the isolation of lockdown. I found myself spending a lot of time remembering and mulling over my career and decisions and outcomes. I wouldn't normally be given to reminiscing and reviewing, but lockdown had a huge effect on me in that regard. When the present was so shut down and life so narrowly defined, the past took on a more vibrant hue. It became more real in many ways, and I gave myself over to it in a most uncharacteristic fashion.

Naturally, there are various ideas of justice and how to deliver it, but my own took shape in the courtroom, from the vantage point of the judge's bench. There is a common perception that a judge relies on instinct, or a hunch. I think that over time a judge does develop a good nose for truth and lies, and experience proves a trusty ally. But that nose is far from infallible, and I don't believe there is some sort of magical hunch or wisdom that is bestowed upon a judge over the course of their career. The one time that stands out for me where instinct played a role was during the hearing of an allegation of abuse against Fr Tony Walsh. A solicitor later described my decision to convict Walsh as 'inspired'. It did involve gut instinct, but it wasn't just a hunch. That decision was also based on listening intently, watching intently and deriving every piece of 'evidence' I could from the accused's demeanour and reactions to the complainant. It was solidly based on what I could hear with my ears and see with my eyes, so any inspiration was based on empirical evidence.

I would have deplored a situation where there was a constant need to be inspired in order to reach a judgment – give me facts and hard evidence any day. As judge, your decision has huge consequences for all concerned, so you don't want to base it on a hunch. You must seek out all the evidence that is there: from the Book of Evidence, from body language and from the words and actions of all concerned – accused, victim, legal representatives, gardaí and probation officers. The verdict is the culmination of the work of many people, so to do it justice it is necessary to take into account every available shred of evidence. I certainly didn't want to hand down verdicts based solely on what my own gut was telling me – that would have felt like a derogation of my duty.

In essence, the judge must decide between two right versions, since both parties consider their version of events to be accurate and fair. Sitting on the bench, you soon learn that some people are excellent at delivering totally untrue 'facts' with disarming confidence. That is very difficult to navigate. This is where experience can prove an ally. You learn how to listen, how to observe, how to read the Book of Evidence and you note even minor details. You're alive to anything that might give you pause and make you think twice, because those little details can be enlightening. For example, a witness might say something in the dock that contradicts something tiny in the Book of Evidence, but it's enough to ring alarm bells. This is why I think the ability to listen is the greatest skill a judge can possess.

This links to my belief that justice can only be applied on a case-by-case basis. There is no menu on the door of the court suggesting that X act equals Y sentence. There is no single level of justice. There might be minimum sentences applicable for certain crimes, but the court and the judge must apply justice according to the merits of each case and according to the behaviour of the accused, past and present. This is an important point. We often hear that everyone is equal before the law, but that equality exists only until the court finds the defendant guilty or not guilty. If the finding is guilty, then the person's past behaviour must be taken into account. Say, for example, Person A and Person B each steal a car and are brought before the court. It's the same offence, so does justice mean they receive the same judgment? No. The judge hears the offence, decides the question of guilt, and then examines the backgrounds of each and whether there are previous convictions. You're as equal as your convictions, so if Person A has no priors and Person B has 10 priors, then equality goes out the door. The judgment on Person B will likely be a prison sentence, whereas for Person A it might be a request for a probation report and alternatives to prison. That's the foundation of each verdict: considering all relevant details and then basing judgment on the broader picture in order to arrive at a decision that is just and fair in those particular circumstances.

My own conclusion was that justice ought to look at the whole person, rather than simply at the crime. I think we should examine all of the circumstances, and we should do so by listening to both sides of the story. That said, it is often difficult to balance the justice sought by the accused with that sought by the victim. It is not always possible for the judge to give the victim the justice they would like to see administered. For example, if a car is damaged by an accused who is on social welfare and cannot afford to pay to repair the damage, while the victim may be pleased to see a prison sentence handed down, they may have preferred to have their car repaired – they may see that as more 'just' and therefore more satisfying. Each person in court may hold a different idea of what justice is in their case, and as judge you cannot deliver on every idea. It's about balancing the scales – as we always picture justice to be – and trying to ensure both sides feel they have been dealt with fairly and that there is a resolution to the matter.

The conflict at the heart of justice – between the needs of each party involved – is one reason why I would strongly support restorative justice. It wasn't much of an option during my career. Although I can see the potential problems inherent in it, particularly that it's usually a very slow process, I think it's a very worthy form of justice with the potential to deliver long-term benefits. Restorative justice entails the court, gardaí and Probation Service mediating between the victim and the accused to promote understanding and contrition on one side and understanding and forgiveness on the other. It is a learning experience for both parties, and I think that could prove extremely productive.

I witnessed restorative justice in action in Tallaght, in 2004. The case involved a young man who had stolen a handbag. The victim bravely agreed to try this form of justice and committed to engaging with it. The young man wrote her a letter of apology, which initially would have been the furthest possible action from his mind. Eventually, they met face to face and talked. He learned what the crime had meant to her, and she learned what had led him to do it. This is something that often struck me on the bench – how the accused generally had no notion of what their crime meant to their victims. I watched that play out again and again – when they heard the victim's version and the consequences for them, they were sometimes astounded and often chastened. In the case in Tallaght, the young man got the opportunity to learn about what he had done, which obviously included the opportunity to choose not to reoffend. This type of justice is based on hope, which is a powerful concept.

On the bench, I was a great believer that prison wasn't always the solution, and that it was often far preferable to try to get the accused out of the criminal mindset, if that was possible, without in any way lessening the trauma to the victim. This was why I judged each case individually, basing my judgment on, among other things, the accused, their criminal background and their attitude. I was led by the belief that if other forms of justice, such as restorative justice or community service or probation, could lead the accused out of a life of crime and into decent society, that was the very best outcome for all parties – those in court and the wider society outside the court. Yes, it made the process longer and more intricate, but justice is often a long-term process rather than a quick-fix Band-Aid. That said, I'm also well aware that not every victim will be receptive to the idea of alternatives, particularly restorative justice, and I wouldn't criticise those who couldn't countenance it. But it is right and good that it is at the court's disposal, and I would hope to see that option become more embedded in the coming years as a strong and fair form of justice.

However, I was at a Zoom conference hosted by Le Chéile Peer Support Project in Limerick in November 2021, and while the discussions were insightful and encouraging, it was also clear that we have a long way to go before restorative justice can be a common option available to the court. We were shown a video in which local people were asked about restorative justice and whether they would consider using it. I loved the honesty of the answers and the respondents' openness to the idea. It seemed very promising. But the video concluded with the fact that restorative justice has barely taken off in this country. Having witnessed it in action in the case in Tallaght, I can understand why. It requires huge patience, huge resources and time. In other words, it would require a complete overhaul of the current system to implement it properly. That's why I was saddened but not surprised to hear that it wasn't widely available.

I suppose you would have to ask if justice depends on a good judge. It certainly depends on an engaged, informed and open-minded judge presiding. The next question then must be: what makes a good judge? I don't feel qualified to answer that and feel it would be impudent to attempt to define it. A judge is a human being, and we are all different and none of us thinks exactly alike. We have legal precedents to help guide our judgments, but so much is based on our assessment of the situation and the people involved, and that's subjective – aside from the facts and evidence of the case. I think the better way to look at it is that there are good judgments and that the judge is in service to the judgment. There will be a judgment that fits the crime and the experience of the victim, and the judge's task is to arrive safely at it through observation and understanding. The biggest compliment I could give to any judge is that they heard and understood – in this way, justice is served.

The point of the judge is to take on the responsibility of deciding on and delivering the verdict.
To my mind, that responsibility demands that the
judge engage fully with all the facts of the case as
well as with the people presenting the case. That is
my concept of justice. However, I do wonder now
if that concept is based in large part on my personality. Going back to *The Irish District Court* book
that so incensed me when I first read it, it suggests
that there were judges who administered the letter
of the law but did little else. In my view, a judge
ought to do more than simply administer the law.
A judge could draw up a menu for the door of
the court and give everyone the same sentence
per that decree, and that could be interpreted as
the law, as justice, but it wouldn't do for me. I
believed it was also my duty to find out why the
crime was committed, and then work from there
to the best solution for that individual case. By
my own observation, a judge who doesn't talk
to the accused is far more likely to give a prison
sentence. I think justice should push beyond that
to include the reasons and circumstances that led

to the crime in order to establish if there is a wider justice that can be served. The greatest justice is to acknowledge the victim and help to heal their trauma, and to ensure that the accused never commits a crime again. That is the ambitious goal justice should aspire to achieve.

I do think that my gender played a role in my thinking. From my early days, I could see that I often came at it differently from my male colleagues. At the time, that was not always viewed favourably – hence the nicknames behind my back. But I have lately heard from former colleagues who now say that they did appreciate my way of thinking. Of course, many would still totally disagree with it, but I won't lose any sleep over them. I am not arguing that my thinking was better because I was a woman, though. What I'm arguing is that men and women working together and learning from each other is the best-case scenario, both inside and outside the courtroom. The court can benefit from the dynamic between the differing approaches. I think this is proving to be the case now that there are so many women joining the profession, and hopefully it will continue to do so.

Looking back at my career now, I'm developing a new understanding of the kind of judge I was and why. I was as capable of getting things wrong as the next judge – and time has shown me that I did get some decisions wrong – but I think my upbringing and personality were brought to bear on my approach to my work. It now makes sense to me why addiction and places like Tiglin and St James's Camino are so dear to my heart. When I look at it, they encapsulate all of the key elements of my preferred style as a judge: talking to the accused as an equal, giving second chances, being there to applaud those who take that second chance, speaking honestly both publicly and privately, and defying the comfort zone in order to go out, talk to people, give speeches and try to highlight the alternatives to prison – in essence, being fully engaged and interested and curious. I felt a natural kinship with those encumbered by addiction and with those working so hard to help them because I've known addiction, and I've always known, deep down, that my life could so easily have taken a different turn, that I might have become the drowning person who needed the life ring to be thrown at the right moment. Kinship and hope – perhaps those are the two pillars on which my work as a judge rested?

What's interesting to me now is how I'm observing the same truism in the older lives of my peers – that time delivers the verdict on your personal decisions as well as your professional ones. I always used to say that my one regret in life was that I never got to study psychology, and I remember a probation officer one day saying to me, 'But sure, you didn't have to do psychology, you're doing it in court everyday.' When I was a young woman, it was an iron-clad belief that women didn't need psychologists, they just needed to embrace the kitchen sink and get on with it. But I've seen so many people benefit from the help of a good psychologist that I have a huge admiration for the profession. I can understand why those who have travelled the hard road of counselling often decide that they want to reach back and help others, because they are so appreciative of its effect within their own lives. That initial decision – to raise their hand for help – creates a line of interlinked decisions that often culminates in the choice to work for the good of others. I've seen that time and again among former addicts, who routinely drop the ladder back down for those wishing to come up behind them.

I dealt in law and justice, but there's life justice, too – that becomes more apparent the longer you live. If you make poor decisions in life or hurt people, it has a funny way of biting you on the bum later on. We make decisions throughout our lives and perhaps see them as done and dusted in the moment they are made, but that's not always the case. I see it now particularly among my peers who are alone, who don't have strong friend or family networks to support them now that they need them most. When you dig into the why, you'll often find that choices made earlier in their lives are coming home to roost now. It's very sad, but I suppose it's human nature.

I don't think many of us think in terms of legacy as we live our lives – we are so given over to the present moment, the present crisis, the present opportunity that we might not notice those life patterns our choices are weaving. But again, each and every decision does add up in the end to show the world who we were, or who we tried to be. I was struck, for example, by the deaths of Seán

FitzPatrick, Chairman of Anglo Irish Bank, and Austin Currie, a civil rights activist and former government minister, who died one day apart in 2021, FitzPatrick on 8 November and Currie on the 9th. The legacy of those two men epitomises this idea that life justice is waiting for us at the end. The coverage of FitzPatrick was muted, shot through with the legacy of his poor professional decisions. In the end, those decisions have become part of the person he was seen to be, which must have been hard to bear in the years before his death but will likely never be expunged. By contrast, there was a warm outpouring of respect for Currie, whose achievements were itemised as bestowing an honourable and lasting legacy. His decisions had stacked up to show him as a man of integrity, which is the highest accolade most of us could hope to achieve. As I listened to the radio coverage of both men's lives and deaths, I thought to myself that Austin Currie was almost cruel to die within a day and show up Seán FitzPatrick's choices so comprehensively.

For me, I made the decision to remain single, even though my marriage ended when I was only

35 years old. I could have sought out a new life companion, but I was very sure that was not the right choice for me. I knew I was an independent-minded person, that I enjoyed my freedom and that I wanted to devote myself to my work and all the projects that caught my interest. I was asked again and again if I wanted to meet someone or if I was lonely, but nothing could have been further from the truth. I have always been very happy in my own company, and I have always tended carefully to my wide circle of friends. If I had been in a long-term relationship, that might not have been the case. Single motherhood is often frowned upon, but for me it was a blessing, and it was essential to me living my life as I wished to live it. I was free to choose whatever I wished, and to do so every single day of my life. That has been the key to my happiness – and, I think, to my longevity.

I am terribly glad to be able to say now that time has delivered its verdicts on my personal and professional decisions, and I can live with them very happily. Finally, that's what matters the most.

EPILOGUE

YOU DON'T ALWAYS BECOME
WHO YOU EXPECTED TO BE

The bench taught me about life and people –
and about myself. It was an incredibly interesting experience, and I miss it still, even
though my life remains full and work-focused. The
daily life of Kilmainham Courthouse was wonderful
to behold, and I feel very lucky that I got to spend 16
years there as District Court judge. I didn't expect
to become a solicitor – I thought I was headed for
a life in music. I didn't expect to become a judge –
that wasn't even in wildest-dreams territory for me,

not on my radar at all. And I certainly didn't expect to become a judge on the criminal bench, one of the very few women judges working full-time on the criminal side at that time. No one was more surprised than me that this turned out to be my life. I'm not who I expected to become, which is a strange thought, but it also makes me feel grateful.

I'd never have thought of me in my eighties having this mindset, and my young self would be surprised if she could see me. My work and everyone I met connected with it improved my understanding and outlook, giving me a life more interesting than I would have experienced otherwise. I think the key for me was learning to embrace all of life's experiences and to roll with them. I hope that is the case to this day. It's certainly what I aim for every day – to remain open and curious and alive to all that remains to be learned. That is crucial to staying young and engaged with the present world. Life is a learning process, but it is up to us how much we learn – or don't learn. I've seen so many people who shut down around the age of 50, closed their minds and acted as if it was job done. I didn't do that. I plan never to do that.

Our attitudes should evolve and change over the course of our lives, and I believe that should continue until the day we die. My job taught me so much that I would never have understood if I'd been in a different walk of life. I learned about other lives that were entirely alien to me, which led me to understand things I would never have been exposed to if I hadn't ended up as a judge. My own thinking and attitudes were challenged constantly as I came into contact with people who had such different life experiences from my own. If you are genuinely curious about other people and the parameters of their lives, it breaks you out of the parameters of your own. I came from an Ireland that was rigid in its expectations, a social straitjacket in so many ways, but I feel that my work gave me the means to sever those binds and move far beyond my expected course. I grabbed that opportunity with both hands and never looked back.

It is unfortunate that fear holds so many people back from doing so many things. I feared making mistakes, but once I'd made them, I realised it was necessary and useful to misstep and learn from that. We all make mistakes – the person who says they don't is a fool. One of the benefits of ageing is that it brings a certain freedom, because you're more comfortable in yourself. I always had the freedom to be able to apologise, and I treasured that. I once apologised to an accused in the dock. It wasn't about a matter of consequence, but it would have weighed on my mind if I hadn't made the apology. I enjoyed feeling there were no constraints on my behaviour, save those I chose for myself. I was free to think my own thoughts and behave as I saw fit, including apologising when the circumstances demanded it. This is why I don't have any regrets. If I hadn't spoken my mind throughout my life, I think I would harbour regrets, but I don't. I'm happy in myself. Why would I sit here worrying about what's done?

Age brings wonderful benefits, but naturally it brings disadvantages as well. The main difficulty – besides the battle to maintain good health – is the ageism of others. When you are a woman, this is compounded by assumptions centred around your gender as well. I remember I was in hospital a few years ago for a hip operation, and two male nurses were in attendance. I was chatting with one of them when the anaesthetist came in and said, 'You mustn't be a good judge of character if you're talking to him.' I smiled and said, 'That's funny, because I was a judge.' With that, the whole atmosphere changed. I was suddenly treated with a new respect. It was interesting to observe. I moved out of the box marked 'elderly lady' and into the box marked 'former judge', and that changed their attitude towards me. It's amazing how often that happens – although long retired, my job still has the currency to buy me some respect. But really it should not be that way. I feel I ought to receive respect regardless of what I did. I should receive respect for who I am as a person. But that seems to fade as you gather wrinkles and grey hairs, which is a sad thing for all of us.

But certainly, I'm one of the lucky ones, because I have made it to old age and get to enjoy this phase of life. At 84, I've attended many funerals and lost many friends and colleagues. I've said before that judges have it easier than others in court, and this is borne out by the fact that there is a relatively high suicide and early death rate among some members of An Garda Síochána, but not so among judges. The gardaí have an incredibly tough job, and it takes a heavy toll. I attended the funeral of the chief superintendent who was involved in the Regency Hotel assassination case and who later was found dead in his office from a self-inflicted gunshot wound. It was a funeral I will never forget. The chief was respected by so many and there was a massive attendance. I had never seen the like of it before, and I haven't seen the like of it since. There are too few resources in place to help gardaí who are suffering with stress and depression. Their job is massively stressful, but they are largely expected to get on with it. Another funeral was that of a garda who died by suicide after meticulously sorting all his financial affairs, leaving his wife with a clean slate. The calm and rational approach of that devastating act really struck me. Time and again, I have been witness to premature loss of life and thanked my lucky stars that I got dealt a hand of cards that was easy enough to play.

Life teaches us, but only if we're prepared to listen. I know everyone talks of nature and nurture and their roles in who we are and who we turn out to be, but I think there are three elements, not two:

nature, nurture and making the choice to learn. It's not only about things beyond our control, it's also about that which we can control – our willingness to engage, to respond, to learn. That, I think, is a choice. I find that heartening and encouraging, because I know nature and nurture were there in spades with me. Looking back across my life now, I'm struck again and again by the extent to which being an only child in that particular generation formed me. I was at odds with the norms of the times as an only child, and my father was a very strict man who exerted his will over our little family. However, in spite of my fears, that didn't define my entire life. Childhood does last a lifetime, as is often noted, but it doesn't have to set down a rule that may never be broken. The wonderful thing about learning is that you can use it to change the rules – and break them.

I have mentioned before how words can stick fast to a person and never leave them. This was the case for me with certain things my father said to me repeatedly. I held tight on to his admonition – 'Open your mind, you bloody little fool' – every time I tried to do creative writing for school. That became like a kind of mantra within me, like a bell that would toll my imminent failure if I ever tried to do anything I deemed 'creative'. It was a rule I lived by, as I thought, and one I felt incapable of changing or breaking. But the funny thing is that now, reviewing my life as I am in these pages, I have realised that it didn't define me as I always thought it had. Yes, the words stayed with me all my life, and I thought they prevented me from doing certain things, but I can see a different perspective now. I never did become a novelist, no, but I did employ creative problem-solving in my work, in examining cases and arriving at judgments. I can see now that I strived to develop a concept of justice as a dynamic force, not a staid notion. I was flexible in my approach and willing to try alternatives and give people a chance. That was a creative approach. So while I thought all along that my life was shaped by my father's words and opinion of me, I now understand it differently. That's quite a revelation.

Over the last year, while enduring lockdown and working on this book, I have thought and said aloud things I have never thought or said aloud before. That seems impossible when I've had 84 years to think and say, but there you go – there are always new things to discover about oneself, which is interesting. I have found a new honesty to assess my life, and it has thrown up some unexpected truths that escaped my conscious awareness until now. I have come to realise that my desire to help – by which I mean the way in which I conducted my court and the way in which I joined boards and supported projects – stems from my personal lack of joy at times in my life. My childhood was tough, as were my marriage and separation. I can relate to misery. I never saw it before, but I now think that I endured misery, and then I took the second chance afforded to me by marital separation and a working life. I transformed my life and myself, and I was then filled with a desire to help others. I did the very thing I admire so much in the reformed addicts whose graduations and weddings and christenings I attend regularly. That has come as a surprise to me, to frame my life in those terms, but I think it fits. I never would have imagined feeling this way, but I feel immense gratitude to my father and my former husband for the adversity they brought into my life, because it made me stronger and, from that, ultimately, it made me happier.

One thing I can relate back from the vanguard is that it's extremely interesting how time collapses in face of the deepest emotions. When I think about the past, it's like it rises up before me, as vivid as if it were happening now. I've learned that time doesn't give you immunisation from your feelings, because they are part of you, part of the rich fabric of your life experiences. But time does blur the sharp edges of those feelings, so you aren't cut as deeply by them as you are at the time they occur. You can withstand the looking back and, as with everything in life, you can learn from it. In truth, you are everything you have ever experienced, and that is a good thing.

I can appreciate now that my life experiences before I joined the bench informed how I approached the bench and the people brought before me. What once I cast as a negative in fact had very positive consequences as well. The word 'independence' has been threaded through my whole life, and my father really instilled that in me by how he raised me. I became self-reliant and resilient. So when I, for example, marched past the cells and the roars of abuse from the prisoners rolled off me like water off a duck's back, that was the only child in me relying on herself and listening to no one, happy to keep her own counsel. I think I was self-reliant long before I ever realised it. Not having siblings, I had to learn to stand up for myself, to fight my own battles, to think for myself – all the qualities that came in so useful when I served as a judge. The very things I had seen as negatives – that I was alone in the world, bearing the full force of my parents' attention and hopes and fears – were in fact positives once put towards a useful end. I would have had a very different attitude to life – and to my work – if I'd had a different home environment. So now I'm glad for what I had, even if I didn't feel like that at the time.

Naturally, I think back over my career, the kind of judge I was, and what I did and didn't achieve, but I wouldn't be prepared to judge myself on that score. It's for others to judge me, I think. If you asked about, I reckon you'd get very mixed reviews of me, but I would hope that the main feedback would be that I was strict but fair. As a judge, I saw myself as being no different than anyone else, other than having a law degree. But in my early days, in particular, judges, like medical consultants and academics, were regarded and treated as superior.

That is changing, but there is still a way to go. However, as far as I'm concerned, I'm no different from any ordinary Joe Bloggs. I had a wonderful, challenging, sometimes difficult job, and I did it to the best of my ability. When the successes came, when someone turned from the path they were on to a better one, it was never my doing: it was down to them. I just looked on with admiration and respect. That was always, and remains, the very best thing about being a judge: getting to witness the life changes that meant you never saw a particular person again in your courtroom. Between them standing before me and them living a different life was the space in which they changed. I loved witnessing that.

I know there is much wrong with the system, I know that more supports are needed, that mental health facilities are inadequate and that much of our legislation is outdated and not fit for purpose, but if I had focused on that, I would have retired even earlier. It would have broken my spirit. Some argue that there is so much wrong with the system, it can't function. I see the brokenness, but I think there is still the opportunity for good decisions, good justice and change. It's like all those people who quietly do good, quietly help others and devote their lives to trying to heal other lives – yes, you can say it's just a drop in the ocean, so why bother? But you have to appreciate that a drop into the ocean still changes the ocean. It's about playing your small part and hoping those individual contributions add up. It takes time and it takes patience, and a smattering of faith to boot. The results are limited, but for those who do get the help they need, it matters hugely. It's life-changing. I'm back to that realisation reached earlier: that kinship and hope were the pillars of my court. Humanity and optimism – we can't lose those.

I do, however, see a barrier to this lovely vision of a good courtroom and a good justice system for a civil society. I run the risk of sounding curmudgeonly, but I've seen the world around the court change, and I feel there is a creeping diminishment of decency across the board in the professional classes. There were bad apples in my youth as well, of course, but as Ireland rides a wave of prosperity, I've watched as money has skewed people's way of thinking and behaving. Money talks louder than ever, and it can be obnoxious. It takes over the discourse and allows people to justify behaviour that should not be justified. I hope this is something that reverses and doesn't become the norm over the long term.

I have already identified compassion and understanding as the key traits of a good judgment, because together they bring empathy and the desire to act on that empathy. It's perfectly acceptable for the victim not to have empathy and not to want to feel compassion, but the court shouldn't operate like that. It is the overseer and has the ability – the responsibility – to move beyond the criminal act to a broader understanding that will allow the judge to identify the best solution in the particular circumstances. Funnily enough, I think one of the most helpful traits as a judge is to be non-judgemental. If you have empathy, if you are willing to find out where people are coming from, if you keep an open mind and treat everyone as your equal, then you won't automatically judge those appearing before you. That's the kind of judge I wanted to be, and the kind of judge I'd want if I ever ended up in court myself.

This open-minded approach is essential in court because those who commit crimes don't come wrapped up in neat packages labelled 'criminal'. Over all my years on the bench, I have met people who looked and behaved like perfect gentlemen and were guilty of terrible crimes, just as I have met people who fit the bill of 'looks dodgy', but who had strong values and were capable of huge generosity and good works. Derry O'Rourke was one of the former, able to behave with impunity with the children in his care because no one suspected a thing. A similar thing happened two years ago, when I met a man in Wexford who happened to know a man who lived in my locality, a gifted musician. The Wexford man passed a comment to me about the musician being a paedophile and facing charges relating to sexual offences against children. For all my talk of not being easily shocked, I was absolutely flummoxed to hear this. I would never, ever have guessed it of this man. It was a good reminder of the lesson to always be aware of your assumptions, their basis and to remain open to changing your mind.

I have to admit, though, I don't think I was born with a wide-open mind. It was the bench that changed me completely. My experiences in the courtroom granted me insight, perspective and a very developed sense of gratitude that I wouldn't have otherwise acquired. They showed me how lucky I had been in my own life, showed me what really matters, and showed me my blessings in stark contrast to the deprivations I so often witnessed in the lives of those who ended up in Kilmainham. I was struck by a moment Sergeant John Hynes once described to me. It was during the investigation of the Roscommon 'House of Horrors' child abuse case, which was gruelling in the extreme. John had spent the day interviewing some of the children involved, and it was incredibly tough to listen to their accounts. He told me that, when he got home that evening, he crept into his children's bedroom and sat at the end of the bed, listening to their steady breathing in the dark. They were safe, well fed and well cared for. That image really struck me because I could understand it so well. When you come into contact with life's dark side, it makes you reappraise, take stock and give thanks. I think this is where my own positive mental resilience stems from, as well as from being an only child who had to rely on herself in all things. It has gifted me a perspective that allows me to be happy.

I attended the retirement party of Sergeant Hynes a few years ago in County Mayo, and another retired detective, John Cribben, came over to me and said, 'Well, you know, Gillian, you'll have a magnificent funeral.' I didn't like the idea of him putting me in a box already, but I took the compliment it housed! He told me that the gardaí held me in as high esteem as I held them, and that there would be many of them there to pay their last respects when the day came. I don't know what the collective noun for gardaí is, but I was touched by the idea of a rake of them turning up to say a last goodbye. I've always been amused by the fact that there are some gardaí who call me Judge to this day. They'll never call me by any other name. I'll take that as a compliment, too.

That remark is perhaps the highest praise for a career on the bench, when you could so easily be hated. And many people do hate me, I'm quite sure – delighted to see the back of me when I left. But I know that of the thousands of people I worked alongside, listened to, thought long and hard about and pronounced judgment on over my 18 years, many would concede that I was a fair and informed judge. That's how I'd like to be remembered. If there is a single crucial lesson in all this, it is one that could be applied inside or outside the courtroom: it is neither fair nor wise to judge people on a single act or moment in their life. You must look further and strive to understand. If we can't understand each other, no good will ever come of it. That drive to understand is at the basis of good judgments, I think, and the mark of a good judge. That, and a bloody good sense of humour.

Taken altogether, these experiences and my thoughts about them point to the fact that it is essential to accept what happens in life and look for the positive in it, where possible. It is also the case that we are learning every day of our lives, if we care to notice and take the instruction. I'm astonished by the amount I've learned in the past year, working on this book. I spent 20 years saying no to all offers of writing a book, and I never expected to undertake this project, but now I've done a complete U-turn. And I am so glad I took it on, because what I've learned has been unexpected and madly interesting. I'm sure it sounds odd to say I'm uncovering new things about myself at the age of 84, but it's true nonetheless.

What I've found is that age doesn't work as I expected. I think I had been taken in by the age and wisdom nonsense, which is probably a form of ageism in itself. There is no straight path to understanding – far from it. I am realising things about my life now, at this age, that I never realised before. I am piecing my life together in a new way, being honest in a new way. It is fascinating to me that all this is occurring at an age when people assume life has nothing left to teach you. I think it's crucial to know that you are learning every single day you are alive, and that you cannot and should not stop doing so. It's an unexpected realisation for me, but growth is constant, learning is daily, life doesn't unwrap itself before your eyes when you hit a certain age and give you self-understanding. No, you're always working at it, working to empathise with those who have wronged you, working to forgive yourself, working to forgive others, working to understand and gain fresh perspectives. It's a lifelong work in progress. Age isn't an end point in the life sense – yes, death is an end point, but until that final end point, you are alive and thinking and changing. Age really isn't what you might expect it to be.

That brings me back to my starting point: I'm not who I expected to be. There was another life there for me, one where I was a wife, a mother and a housewife, one where I didn't work outside the home or step outside my social circle, and one where I, in all likelihood, died at a younger age because the constant tamped-down stress of that life undid me. Now that I'm standing on that terrace, surveying the broad vista of the past, I can see that clearly. If I hadn't faced the end of my marriage, if I hadn't become a single mother, if life hadn't pushed me outside my comfort zone, I would have stayed in that furrow, ploughing furiously towards absolutely nothing at all. That was the other life, the one I almost lived. Back then, if anyone had told me that at 84, this was the life I'd have led, I would have thought they were mad. It's a surprise. But then, life is one surprise after another, really. And I'm so very grateful for that. I've had so many more ups than downs. I feel so supported and looked after. I have so many friends from my work years, and they are still there for me. It's been a wonderful life, and I've so enjoyed it.